The Sandwich Generation:

A Practical Guide For Estate Planning For Those With Elderly Parents And Adult Children

by

Jacqui Brauman

DEDICATION

To my husband, who tolerates my dreams and puts up
with my workaholism. It's all for you.

OTHER BOOKS BY AUTHOR

Jacqui has also written:

<u>Death and Social Media</u>
<u>In Case of Emergency</u>
<u>The Cult of Dissatisfaction</u>
<u>Acres of Diamonds</u>
<u>Steps to Success for Women</u>
<u>Graduate the School of Hard Knocks</u>

Table of Contents

Introduction...1

Chapter 1
Estate Planning Is Not Just For The Elderly 4

Chapter Two
Where There's A Will..8

Chapter Three
Powers of Attorney 12

Chapter Four
Business and Trusts...18

Chapter Five
Reasons to have a Will..30

Chapter Six
Executors 35

Chapter Seven
When simple become complex....................................40

Chapter Eight
Guardians...44

Chapter Nine
Legacy..48

Chapter Ten
Blended families...53

Chapter Eleven
Providing For Education.....................................56

Chapter Twelve
Mutual Wills..59

Chapter Thirteen
Life Interest or "Use and Enjoyment".................61

Chapter Fourteen
Vulnerable Beneficiaries 65

Chapter Fifteen
TDT..71

Chapter Sixteen
Equalising inheritance.......................................75

Chapter Seventeen
Estate proceeds trust...78

Chapter Eighteen
Wills for minors 82

Chapter Nineteen
Superannuation 84

Chapter Twenty
Self-Managed Superannuation Fund ("SMSF"):
Death and Incapacity 91

Chapter Twenty-One
Will Disputes 96

Chapter Twenty-Two
Estoppel...101

Chapter Twenty-Three
Administration of an estate......................................103

Chapter Twenty-Four
Death and taxes 109

Chapter Twenty-Five
Digital Assets, Facebook, Google and iTunes.......112

Chapter Twenty-Six
More Case Studies 118

Chapter Twenty-Seven
How Do I Talk to My Parents?..............................129

How Much Does It Cost? 134

Conclusion..139

About the Author..141

Introduction

You have elderly parents who need more of your attention, and your children are young adults but they are still at home. Or perhaps your adult children have just started having kids of their own and you are on baby-sitting duty regularly. You are stuck between them. You are torn between them. You have obligations to both of them, and you thought you'd have some freedom by now! Just when your children should be grown up and gone, your parents decline and you need to keep an eye on them.

You are the sandwich generation - sandwiched between your children and your parents.

My advice (and it's a bit cliche) is to make sure you look after yourself first! I mean this in more ways than just physically and emotional caring for yourself. I mean you should get your affairs in order. Because if something happens to you, everything revolves around you, and the others won't manage unless you have a proper plan organised.

Take control.

Get your estate planning in order - your Will, your Powers of Attorney, your superannuation, your instructions about your medical care, instructions about your funeral, and have all your main paperwork in one place, including copies of all your usernames and passwords for all your digital accounts.

Once you have your own Will and Enduring Powers of Attorney organised, and you have left lists about who should get what, and you have made a detailed record of all your online accounts, and your funeral insurance is organised … then you can make sure you talk to your parents about their estate plan.

With your parents, you will want to make sure that any Centrelink benefits they may be entitled to are preserved if one dies. You will want to start considering how they will pay for their aged care. And, somewhat selfishly (but it's okay to think about yourself), you will want to make sure that your inheritance will be structured in a way that best suits your own situation.

Then, drag your children along to an appointment with your solicitor and make sure they do their Wills and Enduring Powers of Attorney. For young people, their superannuation is usually their biggest asset, and they need to make sure it will go where they want it to. Usually this takes more than a Will, and a fair bit of thought. Their Will is also important if they have little kids of their own, because they will need to appoint guardians.

You don't want to be left trying to administer the estate of your intestate child (meaning they die without a Will), with a dispute over the superannuation as well - if your child dies without a Will, it can be time consuming and costly.

This book is your guide, as a member of the sandwich generation, about everything you need to know about estate planning for yourself, as well as what you need to make sure your parents and children consider. This book will give you a great starting point to be able to seek out the further advice and guidance to get your planning done properly - to make sure life is easier for everyone.

If you want more specific advice, then you are welcome to contact me, Jacqui Brauman, via my law firm TBA Law.

Chapter 1

Estate Planning Is Not Just For The Elderly

Is estate planning just for the elderly? The simple answer is: NO. But the problem is that whilst it's important for everyone, those that are busy never seem to get around to it.

Whilst there is a greater likelihood that the elderly's estate planning will be implemented, it can actually be more critical to get your estate planning sorted out whilst you're still in your working life. In the earlier stages of life, the impact of your death can be greater because it is generally unexpected, so you do need to take more care in planning for it.

If your adult children have young children (your grandchildren), you really need to express to them how important it is for them to have guardians appointed, or else the decision will be taken out of their hands and made by someone else (not you). Also, when superannuation is probably one of your biggest assets, or one of the biggest assets of your children, you need to make sure it actually ends up with who you want to have it.

I have even written a book with stories of young families that haven't done their estate planning, or haven't done it well enough, and the horror stories that can happen, if you would like to scare your children into doing their estate planning: **In Case of Emergency** at www.tbalaw.com.au/downloads.

Estate planning doesn't just mean your Will, although that is a crucial part of it. Estate planning covers all the following areas, and should involve a collaboration between your lawyer, financial planner and accountant:

- Wills and Powers of Attorney
- Superannuation and Binding Death Benefit Nominations
- Ownership structure of assets
- Taxation considerations

- Testamentary trusts, and

- Life insurance

If you have a family business, family trust, or other entities that you control, it can be more complex. Similarly, if you are in a blended family, or have vulnerable beneficiaries with disabilities in your family, there are other special considerations that need to be taken into account.

Estate planning also deals with situations involving your total or permanent disability or illness. Accidents happen, and young fit people suffer severe injuries whilst playing sport, in car accidents, or even at work. Please don't think that you, or anyone in your family, is invincible.

Chapter Two

Where There's A Will

SBS aired a show on Insight in September 2015 called "Where There's A Will". You can **watch it here**:
https://www.sbs.com.au/news/insight/tvepisode/where-theres-will

The program focused on Will disputes, although one researcher in the audience was firm to say that the majority of Wills aren't disputed. But when they are, about 75% of disputes are successful. They are generally successful because the Court doesn't actually decide the merits of the dispute, but the parties settle at mediation between themselves. This is still a successful dispute, and I wonder if many of those settlements are a commercial decision to end the dispute and reduce legal fees, rather than the claim having merit.

So, most Wills are not contested. Some in the audience on the program thought there was little point to doing a Will, because it wasn't binding and would be contested anyway. That is a shortsighted view. There are very good reasons to have a Will, and now that the Victorian law has changed (in November 2015), it is more difficult for the Will to be contested so your wishes are more likely to be upheld.

Here are some good reasons to have a Will:

1. Have your say

The primary reason to have a Will is to make sure your hard-earned assets go to whom you want them to go. You will want certain people to benefit from your hard work, and if you don't have a Will your assets are distributed in accordance with the intestacy rules of your State.

Take control.

2. Appoint a guardian for your children

In the SBS program, I was shocked that about 65% of parents with minor children don't have Wills. If you or your adult children don't have a Will, you will not have a valid and binding guardian appointed for any minor children. If something were to happen to your adult children in particular, you should stress to them that they will want to establish who looks after their children (your grandchildren). In the worst case scenarios, the children go into foster care, or there is a Family Court dispute over which grandparent ends up with the children.

3. Specify when someone inherits

As well as saying who your assets go to, you can say when those assets are inherited. The main example would be to children or grandchildren. You might not think your children will be responsible enough to receive their inheritance until they are in their mid-twenties, or even into their thirties. So you can specify this. You can also make some gifts conditional on certain things occurring. If you don't have a Will, all your estate will go straight to beneficiaries outright without any conditions, so long as they are over 18 years of age.

4. Choose who has control

The role of the executor in your Will can be crucial, particularly if assets are held in trust, because your executor will generally be the trustee of that trust.

They will need to be financially responsible people, and you need someone who is good at managing these affairs. If you don't select an executor in your Will, then the person who has the best claim against your estate is the person who is entitled to manage your estate - often this is inappropriate. For example, if you are a single parent then your young children will have the best claim on your estate. Whilst they are minors, it is the other parent that is entitled to manage your estate - you may not want your ex spouse to be the trustee for your children's inheritance.

5. Incur fewer costs

It's like many other things in life - you get what you pay for. Prepare a good Will, and the fees are relatively cheap upfront, and will save you in the long run. It can cost thousands more to manage an estate where there is no Will, or where the Will is poorly drafted or invalid.

Do it right once, and save your family legal costs later.

6. Time

If you have a Will, the time to administer the estate can be dramatically reduced. Although it may still take a few weeks for the estate management to kick in, this is much more preferable to the months it can

take if there is no Will, or if there are mistakes with
the Will.

Chapter Three

Powers of Attorney

There are two primary enduring powers of attorney available in Victoria. One is for medical treatment, and the other covers financial, legal and personal matters. An attorney appointed for you must act in your best interests, but not in the best interests of your other family members or beneficiaries of your estate. They are "enduring powers" because they continue after you have lost mental capacity, but you are still alive.

Clearly, these are important for elderly people who are declining in physical or mental ability. But they are also important for young people, in case they have an accident and become physically incapable, or if they are in an induced coma for a period of time. It is also important to do a power of attorney whilst you are well, because once you are unwell, it is too late and a trip to VCAT would be required to ask for an Administration Order.

Selecting your attorney

It should be obvious that you should never select the wrong people to be your attorney, but in determining who is right and wrong for the role, there are some important things to keep in mind. of course you need to choose someone who you trust, or perhaps appoint a number of people that will keep checks and balances on each other. But there are also other things that you need to keep in mind.

You should be realistic in terms of the personality types and relationships between the people you select, and whether you make them joint attorneys, or whether they can act separately. There is no dispute resolution process set out in an enduring power of attorney document, so if you make your appointments work jointly, and they don't agree on something particular, then they will have to go to VCAT to resolve the issue.

Another important aspect to bear in mind when you're selecting the right people to be your attorney, is whether they are even eligible to do so or not. You cannot appoint someone under 18 years of age, which should be obvious. You cannot appoint someone that has been convicted of a fraudulent offence. You also cannot appoint someone who is a care worker employed to care for you, or someone you is providing aged care accommodation to you (or your elderly parents).

Binding Death Benefit Nomination

You should never give the power to your attorney to be able to change your binding death benefit nomination on your superannuation. You have made that binding nomination for a reason, even if someone else doesn't think it's the best decision.

If you do not specifically exclude this power from your attorney, then they automatically have this power under an enduring power of attorney.

You should specifically state in your power of attorney document that your attorney is allowed to renew your binding death benefit nomination, but *not* change or revoke it.

Your Dependants

If you have children or a spouse or other person who is financially dependant, then you should not forget to give your attorney the power to provide funds for these people. If you forget to include this power in your enduring power of attorney document, then it may be contrary to the attorney's powers to use your funds for other people (because on the face of it, it is not in *your* best interests).

Social Media Accounts and Digital Assets

Do not forget that a lot of your life may now be online or stored remotely under the control of an online business. If you forget to specifically give the power to your attorney to deal with these accounts or assets, then some of these business may not recognise the power of attorney at all. The primary reason is that most of these businesses are not based in Australia, and they are not familiar with the board powers that an attorney gets under the enduring power of attorney. It will take a lot of time and effort to convince them that your attorney has the power, unless it is specifically stated in the enduring power of attorney document.

When does power begin?

Enduring powers of attorney for medical purposes don't begin until you cannot made medical decisions for yourself anymore. The other type of enduring power of attorney is the one that gives powers in relation to financial, legal and personal matters. These powers of attorney can begin immediately upon you signing them, or they can be specified to only begin once you have actually lost capacity. This is up to you.

Quite a lot of people ask me how it is determined when capacity is lost, so that the power of attorney begins, particularly in relation to their elderly parents. This is a difficult question, because the definition of 'capacity' is different for different kinds of decisions, and whether it is physical or mental capacity. Capacity is also not exclusively a medical question, because the Courts will not solely consider medical evidence in determining capacity in the event of a dispute.

The best that an attorney can do in making the decision about whether their loved one has lost capacity enough for the power to commence, is to get a medical certificate. If you are the appointed attorney for your elderly parents, and you are in doubt about whether the powers have commenced or not, you could get a referral from their GP to a geriatrician or a neuropsychologist for a report. But if it is fairly certain that there are not going to be any disputes in the family about the use of the power, then a medical certificate should be sufficient.

When an attorney starts to use the Enduring Power of Attorney document, they should provide a certified copy of the document along with the medical certificate to each financial institution the first time they use it. This can then be kept of record, and does not have to be produced every time it is used.

The real issue about capacity only really arises if there is a dispute amongst the family, and other members of the family who don't have any powers have an issue about the use of the power, or whether the power should have commenced or not. Usually such proceedings would commence in VCAT, and VCAT would consider evidence from family members, nurses or other carers, along with medical certificates and specialist reports. VCAT can also order specialist reports to be prepared.

The test as to whether someone has lost capacity enough for an Enduring Power of Attorney to begin is a different test than the test used to determine whether someone has capacity to make a Will.

If you are appointed as an attorney under a power of attorney, please make sure you get advice about your role and responsibilities. Don't mix your funds with those funds that you are administering for your elderly parents. Keep records on what you spend, particularly if you withdraw cash to pay for necessary items. Make sure you only spend money on what is in the best interests of the person who has appointed you, and do not spend any of the money on yourself (do not even allow the person to give you money). More information can be found from the Office of the Public Advocate in Victoria, or the similar department in your State.

Chapter Four

Business and Trusts

Business succession planning is about planning for the future. It is about making sure that your family and employees won't be left in the lurch is something happens to you, if you are running your own business. It is about planning for retirement, and planning for sudden illness, injury or death. It is about making sure your family will not be stressed when they are grieving, as it would be unfair on them to try to fill your shoes.

Business succession planning is also about making sure your business is an asset of some value to your family, instead of the business dying with you.

In 2013, RMIT University completed a report based on a survey of 5,000 randomly selected Australian small businesses. It showed that:

- the average age of the owners was 58

- the proportion of owners who were 65 or older was 25%

- within Australia, Victoria accounted for 35% of the firms (NSW/ACT 42%)

- 60% indicated that the CEO successor would be a family member and that it would be feasible to implement family succession, and

- 75% had not yet formulated a succession plan.

An earlier report, completed in 2006, estimated that the wealth of Australian family firms was $4.3 trillion, with 81% of owners advising that they expected to be retiring in the next 10 years - a transfer of wealth of approximately $3.5 trillion.

So there is a lot of wealth tied up in businesses in Australia - you need to make sure you get the most out of yours.

Planning your exit

Your exit strategy is your succession plan from your small business. For each small business, their succession plan could look different. It could involve, depending on the level of planning:

- outright sale of the business to a third party

- transfer of management to family members, along with some form of ownership control

- sale of the business to a staff management team

- closure of the business because options were not sought early enough, or

- a combination of various elements of the above.

If you want your business succession planning to be successful, my main tips are:

- do it early

- do it openly, and

- do it systematically.

A proper succession plan could take up to 3 to 5 years, depending on its complexity, so the earlier you start, the better. There is no one-size-fits-all. Each business is unique, with its own complexities and personal dynamics. It is important to establish goals and objectives from the beginning, and have a clear focus as you go through the process.

The roadway to succession planning generally has 12 steps, with some steps being more complex than others. Some might be easy and quick for you. Others might take a fair bit of time to implement. Others might need the help from professionals, such as your accountant, financial planner, lawyer or insurance broker. These are roughly the steps:

- set your goals and objectives

- choose your preferred exit strategy and back-up preferences

- get a business valuation

- review your business structure and organisation

- consider tax and legal requirements

- review or set up your estate plan

- begin the process of successor selection

- being the process of successor training

- have a contingency plan, if an emergency happened

- ensure a conflict resolution process is clear

- establish timelines for your successor to take over, and

- have a communication plan.

The legal documents that you may need reviewed or put into place are:

- your start up/business structure documents, such as your company constitution, your shareholder agreement, your trust deed, your partnership agreement, your buy-sell agreement, or a combination of these;

- loan agreements

- contracts for the purchase of assets, and hire agreements

- leases

- insurance policies

- licence agreements, and

- your Will and powers of attorney.

But **step one** is to work out your objectives; what do you want? When do you want to retire? How much do you need to retire? Who do you have in mind to run your business? Do they know of your plans and are they ready?

Then **step two** is to find some professionals (solicitor, accountant and financial planner) that you trust, and who can work together. Put together a bundle of your documents listed above, and **make an appointment** with a solicitor.

You can make the process as quick or as slow as you want, or as complex or simple as is needed. Just do something - don't leave no plan. A business succession checklist is included at the back of this book, to assist you further.

A business succession planning checklist can be found in the Schedule to this book.

Avoiding disputes with a business partner

Not having a buy-sell agreement with your business partner is a critical mistake that so many business owners make. Whether you are partners, shareholders in a company, or unitholders in a unit trust, you should have a buy-sell agreement.

A buy-sell agreement won't completely avoid disputes between you and your business partner, but it will give a framework on how to easily resolve disputes or dissolutions. You will work this framework out together whilst the relationship is rock solid and fine, so neither of you can claim that it is unfair later.

This can be set up as soon as you go into a business relationship, or at any time later in the established business, but particularly during the process of succession planning a buy-sell agreement is useful.

Things that are sometimes assumed at the beginning of a business relationship, that shouldn't be assumed include:

- the date the partnership needs to be reviewed
- describing the partners or shareholders contribution and equity

- establishing how the bank account operates and placing a cap on the cost of decisions

- establishing a limit to personal guarantees

- establishing a dividend and compensation policy

- establishing a policy for a right to inspect the business records and get an audit

- establishing insurance coverage for the partners, and dates when these should be reviewed

- establishing provisions for partners:

  ➢ if they wish to retire

  ➢ if they wish to withdraw equity

  ➢ if they want to expel a partner

  ➢ if they want to sell to an outsider

  ➢ if they lose their professional licence

  ➢ if they go bankrupt

- establish a method of valuing the share of a partner who retires, dies, or becomes permanently disabled

- establish right and options for surviving and remaining partners

- establish non-competition terms

- establishing a dispute resolution process

If you deal with these things up front, then it is less likely that you and your business partner will have a major dispute or falling out that leads to litigation.

Family trusts

A significant number of family businesses are run in family discretionary trusts, so the control and succession of the family trust must be managed. If your business is in a family trust, then this section is relevant for you.

The crucial roles in a family trust are the trustee, the appointor and the guardian (if any). As a quick overview, the trustee runs the trust, the appointor has the ultimate power because they can sack and replace the trustee if they don't like what the trustee is doing, and the guardian needs to give permission on certain types of decisions before things can be done. When 'mum and dad' are in control of the trust, often they are the joint appointors, and they are the trustees, or they have a trustee company of which they are directors and shareholders. These are the roles and powers that need to transfer to the right people if control is going to successfully transfer to the next generation.

So there's no one 'correct' way to transfer the control of your family trust, but of the following options, one of them will be the best way for you:

- you could ensure that the family trust is automatically wound up instead of transferring, but this is rarely the best option because of potential Capital Gains Tax consequences;

- you can ensure that the control of the trustee and appointor roles are transferred to certain people;

- you can make determinations ahead of time to ensure that certain beneficiaries receive a portion of the trust income, and perhaps some capital;

- you can ensure that the guardianship role transfers to a certain person, or insert a guardian role into your trust if it doesn't exist so that someone has the veto power on certain decisions;

- you could amend the trust deed to exclude and/or add certain beneficiaries; or

- you could look to split or clone the trust so that your children don't have to share the trust.

As in most detailed estate planning, everything is a matter of considering the likelihood of the risk of disputes and/or someone acting contrary to your intentions, or contrary to the best interests of all the beneficiaries. Consideration also needs to be given to things that could go wrong, and the cost of addressing all the risks.

Step 1: Know Your Trust Deed

The first step is to get a copy of the trust deed and read it! You need to know what roles are built into the trust, who is appointed to what role, and how the succession of each role works:

- who is the trustee, if the trustee is a company who controls it, and how is the trustee appointed or replaced;

- who is the appointor or principal is, whether it is a joint role, and how the succession works (is there a power of appointment, or is it automatically the legal personal representative?); and

- is there a guardian, what decisions need to be approved by the guardian, and how does the current guardian pass that power on?

Step 2: Know Your Objectives

You probably set up the family trust for tax and wealth planning, particularly for splitting income between a number of beneficiaries. This needed an emphasis on flexibility and complete discretion of decisions to those in control.

But for the purposes of planning the succession of your business, you now need certainty. You need to have control over what entitlements and powers pass to whom, so that the family wealth continues into the next generations, and that disputes don't tear your family apart.

Passing control and certain powers to the right person under the trust is very important.

Wills are effective for assets that you own, but <u>you don't own trust assets</u>. You may have powers of appointment that you can pass under a Will, but you may want to pass some of the control whilst you're alive instead of under your Will. Then you can transition the wealth carefully and not suddenly.

Step 3: Structuring the Transfer

If the trustee is a company, then the power over the trust lies with the board of directors, and it's fundamental that it will operate fairly in the hands of your children. Make sure the constitution of the company allows for each shareholder to appoint a director. Make sure that decisions have to be unanimous, so that an odd child is not always overruled.

Consider winding up the trust on your death, if you do not believe that the next generation can carry on the trust successfully. There will be capital gains tax implications, and potentially other asset protection problems with placing the assets directly in the hands of the next generation, but these could be managed through your Will.

Or consider splitting or cloning your trust. There are other structural considerations that can be explored, so long as you know what your objectives are.

Despite the day-to-day decisions in the trust being controlled by the trustee, remember that the appointor or principal of the trust controls the trustee, and can sack the trustee if they don't like what they're doing. This power is crucial, and who it passes to must be considered so that the control of the trust is fair.

Step 4: Changes to the Trust

As well as considering the overall structure, you may need to consider tweaking some of the details in your trust deed, whether to change the categories of beneficiaries, or how some of the powers work, or even enhancing the powers of the guardian so that certain decisions need the guardian's approval before the trustee can proceed. If you are considering one child having control of the trustee, maybe you want all your other children to be joint guardians, so they all have to agree on the bigger decisions.

The moral of this chapter (in fact, the entire book): don't sit back and hope for the best. Take control of your wealth, and know how your trust works. Then work out what you want to happen and consult a professional that can help you achieve what you want.

Chapter Five

Reasons to have a Will

There is no obligation to make a Will, but having a Will offers many benefits, both financial and personal. It can help take some of the stress and worry off your spouse, children and loved ones in the event that you do die. Likewise, encouraging your parents and your children to have Wills can take stress and worry off you, because you know that their wishes are outlined in a way that will take a lot of uncertainty out of the process.

Have your say

The primary reason to have a Will is to make sure your hard-earned assets go to whom you want them to go. You will want certain people to benefit for your hard work, and if you don't have a Will your assets are distributed in accordance with the intestacy rules of your State.

Having a Will also ensures that you take control over the process as best you can, and ensure that the right people are managing your affairs so that your wishes are going to be carried out in the best way possible. The same can be explained to your parents and your children in relation to their estates.

Specify when someone inherits

As well as saying who your assets go to, you can say *when* those assets are inherited. The main example would be to children, being your grandchildren. You might not think younger people will be responsible enough to receive their inheritance until they are much older than the minimum age of eighteen years, possibility into their mid-twenties or even into their thirties. So you can specify this in your Will. If you don't have a Will, children will automatically inherit at the age of eighteen. This is an important point if you want to leave a legacy to your grandchildren, or you want to make sure your children consider this carefully in their Will.

You could also make other gifts conditional on certain things happening first, or on particular circumstances existing.

Leave people out

If you are a single adult without children, and you die without a Will, your parents will inherit your estate. You might prefer your estate to go to your brothers and sisters, or to a friend, or to your favourite nephew. When you make a Will, you have testamentary freedom to leave your assets to whomever you want. Just be aware that this testamentary freedom is sometimes restricted by State laws that allow people to contest your Will if they are excluded. Without a Will, you cannot trust that your estate will end up in the hands you intend.

Likewise, if you or someone close to you is considering excluding someone from the Will, and you think this person may have a claim against the estate if they were excluded, you should seek legal advice. The law in this area has changed a number of times in the last 20 years, and is likely to continue to change as the moral view held by the community changes. There are ways to otherwise reduce the impact of someone making a claim against a Will, so professional advice needs to be sought. Do not rely on American TV shows to inform you on how to exclude someone from a Will, as the laws are significantly different.

Choose who has control

The role of the executor in your Will can be crucial, particularly if assets are held in trust, because your executor will generally be the trustee of that trust. They will need to be financially responsible people, and you need someone who is good at managing these affairs. If you don't select an executor in your Will, then the person who has the best claim against your estate is the person who is entitled to manage your estate - often this is inappropriate. For example, if one of your children is a single parent then your young grandchildren will have the best claim on your estate. Whilst they are minors, it is the *other parent* that is entitled to manage your estate - your child is unlikely to want their ex spouse to be the trustee for your grandchildren's inheritance.

Incur fewer costs

Estate planning is like many other things in life - you get what you pay for. Prepare a good Will, and the fees are relatively cheap upfront, and will save you in the long run. The cheaper the Will you get, the less likely that proper consideration will be taken into your circumstances. It can cost thousands more to manage an estate where there is no Will, or where the Will is poorly drafted or invalid.

Do it right once, and save your family legal costs later. This can be hard to get across to your parents or your children, who are often all about saving money in the short term. So educating them as much as possible about the consequences of not doing it right can be the best thing you can do (or offer to pay for the legal fees yourself, for your own peace of mind).

Time

If you have a Will, the time to administer the estate can be dramatically reduced. Although it may still take a few weeks for the estate management to kick in, this is much more preferable to the months it can take if there is no Will, or if there are mistakes with the Will.

Chapter Six

Executors

An executor is the person you appoint in your Will to administer your estate after you die. They are also known as your "legal personal representative", and their role often converts to the trustee of your estate, particularly if any of your estate is to be held on trust for a beneficiary.

It is a very important decision as to whom you appoint to manage your estate, as their responsibilities and obligations, and how they carry these out, will determine how well your estate is managed.

This is another important conversation to have, particular with your parents, and particularly if you do not want the responsibility of such a role. If there is going to be a complicated estate distribution, or there is going to be a dispute against the estate, serious consideration should be given to having multiple executors who can act together to support each other through the process.

Duties of Executors and Trustees

The main duties of your executor are:

- make your funeral arrangements

- identify and collect all your assets

- protect your assets (eg. insure them)

- attend to legal formalities (probate usually)

- arrange and prepare income tax returns

- deal with any claims against your estate

- pay all your debts

- distribute your estate to your beneficiaries in accordance with your Will, and

- where trusts are established in your Will, continue the management and administration of those trusts.

Powers of Executors and Trustees

Some powers are given to the executor or trustee under State legislation. Other powers must be given by the Will. These powers can all be modified in the Will to reflect your wishes. Some key powers that need to be thought about include:

- investment powers - what assets would your want your trustee to be able to sell and invest in?

- powers to advance money to minor beneficiaries - it is often important to people making their Will that their children's education is paid for out of their inheritance if they are minors. Do you want this to happen, and do you have any conditions to place on this?

- lending - do you want to give your trustee the power to lend money to beneficiaries?

- use of estate property - is it possible for beneficiaries to make use of assets owned by the estate, such as a holiday home?

Who should you appoint as your Executor?

There are three main groups of people that you could choose your executor from:

- family and friends,

- professionals (eg. lawyers and accountants), and

- trustee companies.

When thinking about who you should appoint as your executor, you should consider your family circumstances (eg. do you have a blended family?), the relationships in your family, who you trust most, along with the following:

- will they charge my estate a fee or commission to act as my executor (even family and friends are able to claim a commission)?

- do they have the time to administer my estate (it can be time consuming and quite burdensome)?

- do they have the business acumen to discharge the duties of an executor and trustee?

- are they likely to outlive you (sometimes appointing someone in the generation above you is not the best choice)?

- are they an Australian resident who lives in the same jurisdiction (State) as the bulk of your assets?

- if you appoint only one person as your executor, then you should consider appointing a substitute executor in case your initial executor predeceases you or cannot act for another reason,

- you cannot appoint more than four people as your executor, and

- if you have young children, you should consider making sure that the guardian for your children is not also the trustee of their inheritance.

The more complex your personal and financial circumstances are, the more appropriate it may be for you to consider the appointment of a professional or a trustee company. But these are issues that can all be worked through your the estate planning process.

Chapter Seven

When simple become complex

Solicitors are loath to call even a 'simple Will' a simple Will these days. There are so many aspects to the wording used that the layman doesn't understand, not to mention the trustee powers that need to be included. But even when a Will is relatively simple, there is usually a lot that has been considered before it has been prepared. Instead, these days, you don't go to a solicitor to prepare a simple Will - these involve your Will Kits or Online Wills.

But when should you expect that a simple Will won't cut it for you? Here are a few scenarios:

Superannuation

Most of us have it these days, and it is often our biggest asset once the life insurance component is also paid. This is particularly the case for your children. Remember, super isn't your asset to deal with under your Will, so there needs to be appropriate planning for it. Potentially some Binding Death Benefit Nominations need to be prepared, and then equalisation clauses used in your Will so that distributions are truly equally after tax.

Self-managed super funds, companies or family trusts

If you have any of these entities, they also add further complexities. The assets owned in these entities aren't yours to deal with through your Will. Your solicitor will need to review the Trust Deeds and Constitution to figure out how control can be passed onto the appropriate person that you want. Sometimes there may have to be changes made to the Deeds so that your wishes can be achieved.

Life interests or other testamentary trusts

As soon as you start to consider leaving money to your minor children, to be held in trust until they reach a certain age, then your Will is no longer simple. There are other management aspects to consider for such as trust, as well as who should manage it until your children reach the specified age, and what it can be used for in the meantime. Likewise with a life interest, the rights under this need to be managed, so your Will cannot be simple.

The most complex trusts are family discretionary testamentary trusts, or special disability trusts if you have a disabled loved one that needs to be cared for.

Wanting to leave someone out of your Will

Serious consideration needs to be given to the consequences here, and potentially far greater estate planning to minimise your estate in the case of a claim. This is not something to do lightly, if you want to avoid litigation.

Assets outside Australia, or even Interstate

Assets outside of the country need to be given special consideration, particularly how the law applies in that country, and how a Will in Australia will apply. But if you also have investment properties in other States within Australia, the law also affects these differently in each State, and there are potential consequences when it comes time to obtain probate, as this may need to be resealed in other jurisdictions.

Making specific gifts or promises to beneficiaries

Sometimes gifts can be straight forward. Other times, consideration needs to be given to how it is done, particular if an estate could have debt, or if the will-maker wants to avoid ademption (where the gift no longer exists). Further, if you make promises to beneficiaries that they may seek to rely on if you don't stick to the promise, these need to be explored thoroughly, particularly if you change your Will later.

Chapter Eight

Guardians

If you have minor children, you can't leave their future uncertain. More importantly, if you have young grandchildren, then you need to express to your children the importance of their Wills. Updating our Wills is usually the item on our 'list of things to do' that never gets done. Quite often, if our Wills aren't up to date, or we don't get the proper advice, our Will doesn't actually protect our children or our loved ones, and there are mistakes.

To make sure you do the best for your children and grandchildren, please consider the following tips when appointing guardians to care for them:

Family members may not be the best choice

We often mistakenly believe that young children would be too much of a burden for our closest friends to raise, if something should happen to us. We think that family is the better option, because family is family, and they are really obliged to do so because of blood. But these beliefs are false.

You need to make the decision about appointing the guardians of your children based on your parenting values, their proximity and (physical and emotional) ability.

Name more than one possible guardian

If you name a couple as the guardians for young children, would you be happy for one of that couple to continue raising your children if they divorced, or if one of them died? The appointment of guardians can be conditional, and an alternative or back-up guardian can also be appointed in case the primary choice is no longer suitable or available.

You don't want to leave it up to the primary guardian to appoint a back up guardian without your input or consent! You also don't want the primary guardian failing in the role and giving the young children up to be cared for by someone else, or the children ending up in a Family Court battle.

Don't base your decision on financial resources

The decision as to whom is appointed as guardian should not be based on money. This is a reason that we often avoid appointing friends rather than family, because we think it will be too much of a financial burden. But, there are arrangements that can be made such that guardians won't be out of pocket raising young children.

The children's inheritance can be utilized for their education and maintenance by the guardian, even before they are old enough to inherit, if this is expressly allowed in the Will.

To make sure this works, the selection of the executor is just as important as the selection of a guardian. You don't want them to be the same person, or to act alone, or there could be a risk of abuse of the access to the children's inheritance. You will want someone in the role of executor who will be financially responsible if you appoint them, and you will want them to understand what you would approve money to be spent on and what you wouldn't (for example, you might not want your executor approving your children's inheritance to be spent on an annual holiday on the Gold Coast for them and their guardian).

Notify the people appointed as guardians and provide them with proper instructions

Make sure you let the people you appoint know! It will be better for your children to know their potential guardians well, and the guardians you have appointed are likely to take a more keen interest in your children.

You also want to document some instructions, if possible. You want to leave behind as much detail as you can, and guidance, so that the guardians for your children aren't guessing about your intentions. A lot of solicitors don't guide their clients through leaving detailed instructions when people prepare their Wills, but I do. Make sure you find a solicitor that can help you with this, or take the time to undertake this yourself.

Chapter Nine

Legacy

What do you mean, there's different types of gifts I can leave in my Will? I'm not talking about leaving money or leaving your stuff. I'm talking about the *way* you leave it to your loved ones in your Will. Hopefully this will give you some food for thought, and gives you the option to do something a bit more creative than just saying they can work it out themselves.

Specific legacy

A specific legacy is relatively simple - you are giving your beneficiary something specific, that you already own. Giving a gift like this severs the gift from the rest of the estate - so the gift gets preference before the payment of debts, which should come from the residue.

An example would be "I give to X all <u>my</u> shares in the National Australia Bank Ltd company" or "I give to X my oil painting of the Australian high country", or "I give to X all my jewellery".

The gift is specific, you own it, and it goes to someone specific. It is possible that the subject matter could increase from the date of your Will to the date you die, as in the gift of shares (you may have more shares when you die). Likewise, it is possible that you don't own the subject matter when you die, for example you may have sold all your shares.

If you no longer own the specific subject matter when you die, the gift is adeemed and the beneficiary does not get anything in its place.

General legacy

A general legacy is usually money - a pecuniary legacy - but they can also relate to specific items. A general legacy is payable out of the residue of the estate, and if it relates to a specific subject matter, you usually don't own it at the time of writing your Will or dying.

An example would be "I give to X 500 shares in the National Australia Bank Ltd company" or "I give to X $50,000".

In both these examples, the funds need to come from the residue of your estate, before your residuary beneficiaries get their share. The cash would be taken from the top of the residue, usually before the payment of debt.

The shares in this example are not owned by you, either when you sign your Will, or when you die. It is a general legacy because it does not refer to "my" shares. You are creating an obligation on your executor to buy 500 shares out of the residue of your estate for the beneficiary.

Note that a beneficiary may elect to take the cash instead of the 500 shares!

Demonstrative legacy

This form of gift is a mixture between a specific and a general legacy. It is a general legacy, usually money, from a specific place. However, you would need to specify in your Will that if the specified fund was not sufficient, whether you didn't want it paid from residue. If the fund is insufficient, then the remainder will automatically be paid from residue, unless you say otherwise.

An example would be "I give X $50,000 from my funds invested with MLC".

This form of gift is a way of isolating a legacy from eating into what you are leaving for your residuary beneficiaries, so long as you specify that the shortfall is not to be made up from the residue. For example, if the MLC fund did not have $50,000 in it when you died, and you'd used most of those funds for your retirement, then the balance would come out of the residue of your estate before debts were paid and distribution of your residue went to your residuary beneficiaries.

Residuary gifts

The residue is everything left over in your estate that is not otherwise dealt with in your Will. It includes the funds and property left over after the payment of debts, administration and funeral expenses, and all the other legacies you give (specific, general and demonstrative).

You can leave your residuary estate to a specific person or named persons, or you can leave your residue to a class of people, such as "my children". It can be equally divided, or you can split it into unequal parts and leave it how you want to.

Residuary gifts of real property (real estate) and personal property should all be dealt with together, and you should try to avoid dealing with them separately. If you have a specific piece of real estate or other property that you want to go to someone specifically, or a group of people specifically, then you should deal with it as a specific gift.

Chapter Ten

Blended families

Estate planning for a blended family can give rise to unique problems. As well as needing to provide for the new spouse, there are also children from the first relationship, as well as children with the new spouse. There is often a level of animosity between the different groups of beneficiaries, as the children from the first marriage might not like the new spouse or new children.

Separation is not the same as divorce. A new marriage invalidates a previous Will, but a new de facto relationship does not. A separation also doesn't invalidate a previous Will. A divorce doesn't completely invalidate a previous Will, but it does act to exclude the ex-spouse from any role or gift under the Will. If you or your children are separated but not divorced, and have not reviewed your Will, *now* is the perfect time to do so.

The most difficult aspect about estate planning for blended families is making sure that all competing interests are balanced to reduce the likelihood of a claim again the estate. This can not always be successfully achieved.

A current spouse, and an ex-spouse who has not had a family law settlement, have strong competing claims against a deceased estate, and will take preference before any children. Generally, in a Will dispute, a spouse should receive a place to live and a nest egg to allow for any contingencies. Preferably, the spouse should be kept in the lifestyle that they are used to, and not have to give anything up.

The other consideration during estate planning, is that if everything is left to the new spouse, the will-maker should realise that their new spouse may have no obligation to the will-maker's children, so their new spouse is unlikely to leave anything in their Will to your children. This is why life interests were so popular for some time - the house and part of the estate were left to the new spouse for life only, and then on the death of the new spouse it was ensured that this went to the children from the first marriage. Life interests have sometimes been found to be insufficient in a Will dispute, and they also raise many other problems for the flexibility of the new spouse as to where they live.

Quite often, it is useful to have non-estate assets to make up the interests of children. Superannuation, life insurance, and joint assets can all be left to spouses or children without forming part of the estate. This also ensures they are removed from any Will dispute.

This raises the issue of minimising the estate itself to make sure there are not many assets available in the case of a dispute. If set up correctly, it can also ensure the inheritance goes to the right person. Family trusts are a vehicle that could be used, but there are stamp duty and capital gains consequences that need to be considered when assets are being moved around.

A mutual will agreement is another contract that can be used between spouses to make sure that a Will is not changed after the first of the spouses dies, so that beneficiaries are not later cut out by the surviving spouse. This is dealt with in Chapter 12.

Every family is unique and different, and needs to be approached individually, depending on the family dynamics involved and the objections of the will-maker.

Chapter Eleven

Providing For Education

If your children have young children, you may have some influence on making sure your grandchildren are educated and that their inheritance is even. You can speak to your own children about their options, but you could even consider setting up an education trust in your own Will which expires on the youngest grandchildren reaching a certain age, and the balance of that education trust going back to your children.

Here's an example:

Russell and Carrie have three children. Their eldest, Hayley, is 10 years older than the two boys, Alex and

Luke. Their estate is worth about $1,000,000. In the Wills they prepare, they leave everything to each other first, and in the case that they both die they set up an education trust of $250,000, and then individual trusts for each of their children for the balance to be split evenly between them.

Lucky they did set up the education trust. They both die when Hayley is 23 years old. She has already finished her education, as Russell and Carrie paid for that whilst they were alive. It would not have been fair for their estate to be split evenly between the three children if Alex and Luke still have to pay for their education. Hayley would have received an advantage.

Instead, $250,000 is set aside in the education trust for Alex and Luke to finish their schooling. The balance of the estate is split evenly. When Alex and Luke have both finished their schooling, the balance left in the education trust gets split evenly between all three kids. That way all three children get the benefit of their education being paid for by their parents, and they also receive an even inheritance.

If you choose to set up an education trust, you could specify what sort of education fees can be paid for out of it. Whether you only want to ensure they finish private school through to their final year, or whether you also want to pay for university fees or trade school fees could also be specified. Such a trust could also have a broader scope and doesn't have to be limited purely to education expenses.

Setting up an education trust to make sure all your grandchildren have an equal opportunity is similar to other equalization clauses that you could use in your Will to make sure your children all get an even inheritance. If you give one child more than the others during your lifetime, you could include a hotch-pot clause to even this out. If you lend money to one child you could include the forgiveness of that debt in your Will as part of their equal share of their inheritance.

Chapter Twelve

Mutual Wills

Ken and Lynn are married. Both are 60 years old and will not be having any more children. Lynn didn't have any kids, but Ken has two adult children by an earlier marriage. Ken wishes to leave all of his estate to Lynn, but on the condition that if she survives him, she will leave the whole of her estate to his two children.

It's easy for them to make mirror image Wills, with Lynn leaving everything to Ken's children after they've both passed away. But Ken is concerned about the possibility that Lynn might change her Will after he dies.

They agree to enter into a Mutual Will Agreement, which is a contract between them that neither will amend their Will without the consent of the other party. If one of them does change their Will after the death of the other, then it is a breach of contract, and the estate of the deceased spouse can take action.

This might seem to solve the problem at the time, and Ken will certainly feel better. Lynn might feel like Ken doesn't trust her, but she would go along with it because she doesn't intend anything else at this point in time.

Potential problems could arise after Ken has died, such as another relative of Lynn's could make a family provision claim against her Will when she dies. The Mutual Will Agreement between Ken and Lynn does not prevent other people from making a claim. Or, Lynn could give away a lot of the property whilst she's alive, so there is not much left for Ken's children anyway.

There are alternative strategies to making a Mutual Will Agreement, like testamentary trusts, and some forms of life interests. Depending on how assets are owned, assets can also be removed from the estate so that they are left directly to children, or asset ownership can be changed from joint proprietor to tenants in common, so that Ken could leave his half of the family home directly to his children instead of to Lynn.

Chapter Thirteen

Life Interest or "Use and Enjoyment"

After you die, you might want a spouse or a child or a parent to have the benefit of a certain asset - like being able to live in a particular house - for the rest of their lives or for another specific period of time. You can achieve this a number of ways in your Will. The first option is to grant a life interest, which was more common in the past than it is now, although life interests have become far more complex and flexible than they used to be. The other main option is to create a "use and enjoyment" trust, and to give the specific person the benefit of that trust.

Let's say that you want to let you second husband live in your house after you die, but you want the house to belong to your children. There are certain events that can trigger the end of the use and enjoyment trust, and even the life interest if it is drafted properly:

- death of your second husband, in which case your children would then be able to use or sell the house,

- your second husband remarries, or forms a de facto relationship,

- your second husband no longer wants to live there so leaves, or perhaps cannot continue to live their due to health reasons.

This list is not a complete list, because you can put all sorts of conditions on such a trust or life interest.

If you want to create such a trust, or a life interest, you should consider who needs to pay the outgoings on the property, who insures the property, and who maintains it. Generally, it is the person you leave the asset too, such as your second husband used in the example above. Terms can also be built into such a trust that if your second husband doesn't pay for things or maintains things properly (remember this house is meant to be your children's inheritance), then your children could either step up and pay, or they could have the option to evict your second husband.

One of the main reasons you would use such a trust, or a life interest, is because you want to make sure your second husband is provided for, but you still want your children to receive their inheritance. If your true intention is to make sure your second husband has somewhere to live, you should also think about the circumstance when he wants to downsize, or if he has to go into a nursing home. Clauses can be built in to allow the property to be sold and part of the proceeds to be used to buy something smaller - the surplus would go to your children, and the smaller property would also be your children's in the long run. The same would apply if the property needed to be sold to raise the money for your second husband to go into a nursing home - surplus would go to your children straight away, and the rest would be used as the bond for the nursing home. When your second husband died, the nursing home would return the bond to your children.

Another alternative would be that instead of the surplus on a sale going straight to your children, you could also specify that it was to be invested and your second husband would be entitled to the interest off that investment, but the capital would be kept for your children once your second husband finally died.

The primary difference between a life interest and a use and enjoyment trust is that the life interest is a proprietary interest in the property, and can have tax consequences. If you are considering an arrangement such as either of these options, then you should get proper tax advice from an accountant as well, to make sure the best option is chosen for your children.

Chapter Fourteen

Vulnerable Beneficiaries

When any of our family members are gamblers, alcoholics, drug-users, bankrupts or have a severe disability, we may be reluctant to leave a direct legacy to them in our Will, out of fear of it being wasted or abused. But we shouldn't avoid leaving anything to these family members, because they are the ones most in need of a legacy. So what can be done? There are a number of things that can be done.

Protective trust

Protective trusts have been legislated - the Victorian version can be found in section 39 of the *Trustee Act 1958*. They are a bit old fashioned. How it works is that you leave the inheritance to your wayward child in a protective trust. <u>Only the income</u> earned from their inheritance can be paid to them, and the whole of the capital is protected. It prevents the wayward child from spending a capital lump sum. After your wayward child dies, the capital part of the inheritance can be passed to someone else of your choosing (maybe your grandchildren, or maybe another child).

These were set up a lot in the 1950s and 1960s, but there has been many that have been contested and set aside, so the child ends up with their inheritance anyway. And there are other problems of trying to forfeit the interest in the protective trust, and when the protective trust ends if not on the death of the child. There is also the issue that any income from the protective trust could still be available to your child's creditors if your child became bankrupt. So whilst the capital is protected, the income is not.

Special Disability Trust

Another alternative, and this trust can be set up whilst you're alive or in your Will, is a Special Disability Trust. It might be appropriate to use this form of trust in combination with another, because you can set this up now instead of waiting until you die.

This trust can be used for a specific person who meets the disability requirement in the *Social Security Act 1991*. There is a gifting concession of $500,000 into a special disability trust, and also the assets of a special disability trust (up to approximately $596,000) are not assessed as assets for Centrelink purposes - so your disabled family member will still retain their full pension.

The requirements of such a trust are pretty stringent, including:

- the trust must be for only one beneficiary,

- the sole purpose of the trust must be to provide for the accommodation and care of the beneficiary,

- the terms and conditions of the trust must be the standard model trust deed published by the government, and

- the trustee must get annual financial statements completed and have an annual independent audit conducted.

The trust deed that must be used is the Model Trust Deed for Specifically Disability Trusts, which is published by the federal government. There is no flexibility, and you cannot draw up your own trust deed.

A better option might be …

Discretionary trust for wayward child

Finally, you can utilise a discretionary trust in your Will - these are often called testamentary trusts (although all trusts set up in a Will are testamentary trusts). A testamentary discretionary trust (TDT), if worded correctly, can achieve what the above trusts can achieve in your Will, and more. For example, if there are more beneficiaries of the testamentary discretionary trust than just your vulnerable family member and the trustee is a responsible person that you trust, then the assets can be protected as effectively as the other previously mentioned trusts from your vulnerable family member.

With a TDT, the trustee can issue income at their discretion to the vulnerable beneficiary and undertake income splitting between beneficiaries, and they can also release capital (unlike a protective trust). Detailed succession clauses can be built in, in case your trustee becomes unable to perform the role or dies, so that you can always be assured of who is in control of the trust. You can also leave detailed instructions to your trustee about what your intentions of the trust are. Finally, you can also build in another role into the trust - the role of protector - which is another independent person who needs to approve of certain decisions before they can occur, if you want that extra level of protection.

Discretionary trust for disabled child

A dTDT in your Will gives you the most flexibility in setting up a trust for your disabled child. Unlike with a vulnerable beneficiary (or wayward child) where that child would be part of a group entitled under a discretionary trust, for your disabled child you would set up an exclusive discretionary trust with your disabled child as the Primary Beneficiary. They would be entitled to the income, and the trust would be managed by someone of your choosing. They would have the discretions that you build into the terms of the trust, so you control what can or cannot be done, and you can leave instructions for the care of your child.

The downside with a discretionary trust is that it could affect your child's entitlement to a full disability support pension. You should plan a discretionary trust with the assistance of both a lawyer and a financial planner, because so long as the capital in the discretionary trust is low enough to still get a partial pension, your child can be better off and still get the benefits of having a pension concession card and health care card.

The next chapter explained TDTs in more detail.

So if you have a child who has problems, the solution is not to leave them out, but to work out a way of protecting them and your hard-earned estate. You need to think about your objectives for your estate and how it would be best inherited by your children, and which trust achieves the best result.

Chapter Fifteen

<u>TDT</u>

A testamentary trust is technically any trust that arises after you die, based on your Will. It could be a minor's trust, a life interest, a protective trust, or a more complex discretionary trust that could benefit your children throughout their lives.

But when you hear people talk about "testamentary trusts", they are generally referred to a family discretionary trust that is set up in your Will. I will refer to this type of trust as a Testamentary Discretionary Trust (TDT) for the rest of this chapter.

A TDT is similar to a family discretionary trust that you might set up whilst you're alive for the purpose of investing or for running a business. A TDT has a trustee and a list of potential beneficiaries - usually the primary beneficiaries are your children. The potential beneficiaries are entitled to receive income and/or capital of the trust at the trustee's discretion, and this could be conditional on your children reaching a particular age. You can set up multiple TDTs in your Will, all with the same conditions, for each of your children.

Like a family discretionary trust, a TDT may also have an appointor and/or a guardian. The power of the appointor is the ability to appoint or remove the trustee to one of the beneficiaries of the trust. This is a crucial role, particular if you initially chose an independent third party to be the trustee, for example, whilst your children are minors. The power of the appointor could then be given to your children once they reach a particular age, so that they then take control of the trust.

The other role is a guardian - it's the guardian's function to oversee some of the more significant decisions that a trustee might make. This role would also be important whilst your children are minors, or even if you want to ensure your adult children don't distribute large amounts of capital to themselves if they have a gambling or other addiction problem.

Benefits of a Testamentary Discretionary Trust

Asset Protection

A TDT can protect assets which a beneficiary inherits, because they don't inherit it directly. Instead it is held in trust for them, and you can determine how much control they have of that trust. This is particularly important if your child or other beneficiary is vulnerable, by being a gambler or having a substance addiction, or even if they have a disability.

A TDT is also useful to protect your beneficiary's inheritance from bankruptcy, so would be a useful tool if any of your children run their own business and you want to make sure their creditors wouldn't have access to this inheritance.

Finally, a TDT can also offer some protection from a property settlement if the relationship between your beneficiary and their spouse breaks down. You don't want your child's inheritance to be split up to their ex-spouse. This protection is limited, and you will need specific legal advice to achieve the most protection possible.

Income Splitting

It is the income splitting capability of a TDT which makes this structure very attractive. Unlike a family discretionary trust which you would set up whilst you're alive, you have attractive tax advantages under a TDT when paying income to a minor (child under 18 years). This is because a minor beneficiary of a

TDT is taxed as an adult, at marginal tax rates - meaning, they are entitled to the tax free threshold (currently $18,200 tax free per annum). Compare this is a family discretionary trust, and a minor is only entitled to $416 tax free and then they are taxed at penalty tax rates.

Below is an example of the tax effectiveness of a Testamentary Discretionary Trust. Tom passes away and has $1,000,000 of personal assets that he leaves in a TDT for his wife Kerry. She is the primary beneficiary, but her two young children are also potential beneficiaries under the TDT, so she can income split income to them from the trust. If Tom didn't set up a TDT for Kerry in his Will, then she wouldn't have been able to take advantage of the tax planning and would lose this additional income.

In this example, because Kerry could split the income with her minor children through the trust, she could take advantage of the tax free threshold and save on tax. This has significantly added to her income throughout the year, so she has more to spend on raising her children.

A TDT can be a valuable addition to your Will, if there is this much cost saving on tax even in one year.

Chapter Sixteen

Equalising inheritance

People will often want their children to have an equal share in their estate, and in giving instructions to prepare their Will like this to a solicitor, many may not consider non-estate assets. If a will-maker truly wants their children to all be treated equally, then they also have to consider:

- pre-death gifts

- the control of an entity that will not pass to the intended people, and

- whether the value of post-death distributions will actually be equal.

An important consideration is superannuation. As I tell my clients, if superannuation is paid directly to children from the superannuation, then they will likely each end up with a different amount because if they are adults, they will be paying tax on the superannuation at different rates in accordance with their individual income.

An equalisation clause in a Will to deal with superannuation is often important, or alternatively, having the superannuation paid into the estate so that the estate pays the tax to ensure an equal distribution thereafter.

Other than superannuation, there are other gifts that might need to be equalised. These include gifts of assets or money whilst the will-maker is alive. A true equalisation of an estate would mean that a hotch-pot clause is inserted in your Will to make sure that any gifts whilst you are alive are also considered.

One problem with hotch-pot clauses is whether a 'time benefit' is to be calculated into the gift, or whether it should just be taken to be the amount at the time of the gift. For example, if one son received $250,000 in 1996 needs to be equalised, does the amount of $250,000 get used, or does the amount of $1,000,000 get used (which is the value of the asset that he could be able to buy with the gift in today's dollars)?

Another gift you could make is to allow a child to use an asset free-of-charge during your life. If one of your children lived in your house for free for 8 years, should this benefit be adjusted?

Finally, people often try to reduce their estates by making gifts during their life, and *do not* want these gifts to be taken into account under an equalisation clause. At the time they did their Will, if they included an equalisation clause, they need to understand that any subsequent gifts will also be included into that clause. If you put an equalisation clause into you Will, hopefully you don't forget about it and make subsequent gifts that you don't intend to be equalised.

So, whilst trying to ensure your children are treated equally is an admirable aim, often the actual effect to trying to achieve this is not fully understood either by the solicitor drafting the equalisation clause, or sometimes the will-maker forgets how it works. This can be quite technical, and both solicitor and will-maker need to understand the full intent.

Chapter Seventeen

Estate proceeds trust

In this example, Sara's husband Tim has died in an accident. They have two primary school aged children, Michael and Melissa. Tim and Sara had prepared Wills a few years prior, when the children were still very young. They were basic Wills, which simply ensured that everything went to each other in the case that either of them passed away, and if they both passed away, then their estate would be divided between their children.

Sara and Tim own a house with a mortgage - they owned this jointly, so that the house automatically transfers to the survivor. They have a car each and superannuation. Tim owns a portfolio of shares. Sara works as a teacher, and Tim had a job in corporate finance. Tim also had a life insurance policy of $500,000.

Tim's estate comprises of his share portfolio, the proceeds from his life insurance policy, a payout from his employee entitlements, and his car. His superannuation is paid directly to Sara, and doesn't form part of his estate. The house doesn't form part of the estate, either, as it automatically transfers to Sara as the surviving joint owner. All their other bank accounts were joint account, so they also don't form part of the estate, and are automatically transferred to Sara as the surviving joint account holder. Sara uses the superannuation to pay the mortgage, and has enough left over to invest some for her future. Tim's estate is worth approximately $650,000.

Sara has a couple of options. She could just inherit the estate in accordance with the wishes in Tim's Will. Alternatively, because she doesn't really need the money from the estate, she could set up estate proceeds trusts for Michael and Melissa, so that their future gets a kick start.

An estate proceeds trust can be set up by a beneficiary under a Will for a minor who didn't inherit under the Will, but who would have been entitled to inherit if the person had died without a Will (intestate).

If Tim had died intestate, then Michael and Melissa would have each been entitled to about $183,000 each under Victorian law (check the intestacy laws in your State).

Sara decides that she will set up estate proceeds trusts for each of her children, and transfers $183,000 into an estate proceeds trust for each Michael and Melissa. Under the terms of the trust, they would normally inherit when they were 18 years old, but Sara extends this until they are 25 years old. She invests each sum, and earns about $10,000 per year income from the investment. This income is distributed to Michael and Melissa, for Sara to make use of for their education and other expenses. This income is tax free, because Michael and Melissa are taxed as adults (at marginal rates) on income from the estate proceeds trust (unlike a usual family trust, under which minors are taxed at penalty rates), and they are under the tax-free threshold. So effectively, Sara has given herself $20,000 of extra income per year, tax free, which she can use for the children.

If Sara had kept the inheritance herself and invested it, she would be paying tax on the interest income that it earned. But because she chose to set up estate proceeds trusts for her minor children, she is advancing her children's future and also getting a substantial tax saving.

If you happen to be in such a horrible situation as to lose your spouse whilst your children are young, if is worthwhile taking some time to grieve before deciding how the estate is to be dealt with. You do have 3 years from the date of death of your spouse in which to set up estate proceeds trusts for your children, so don't act too rashly and take your time to plan what is best for you and your children.

Chapter Eighteen

Wills for minors

Ben lives with his mother and step-father. He is sixteen, and is a tennis star on the amateur circuit. He has already accumulated significant wealth through his sponsorship deals and prize money, and this is only likely to continue over the next two years at least.

Generally, you need to be eighteen years old (no longer a minor) to make a valid Will.

If Ben dies as a minor without a Will, then intestacy laws will apply to his estate and all his earnings.

Under intestacy laws, as he has no children, his estate would all go to his parents equally.

Ben's mother and father separated when Ben was too young to remember. His father has been absent for most of Ben's life, until Ben started to become successful and his father started trying to insert himself back into Ben's life. Ben brutally put his father back in his place, seeing his father for the money-grabber that he is, and doesn't want anything to do with him.

Ben doesn't want half of his estate to go to his father, if he dies. He wants to make a Will to leave most to his mother, but to also put some aside for his younger half-sister.

With his mother's help, Ben could apply to the Supreme Court for an Order enabling him to make a Will, under which he could then appoint his mother as his executor, set up a trust for his sister to leave money for her future, and leave the rest to his mother for supporting him during his lifetime.

Most States of Australia have laws to allow minors to make Wills, if this is similar to your children or grandchildren, so please seek relevant advice in your State.

Chapter Nineteen

Superannuation

19.1 Super is not your asset

For many people, their superannuation is their biggest asset. However, your superannuation is not an estate asset to be dealt with under your Will. Instead, it is an asset held on your behalf by the trustee of your superannuation fund. The trustee is the one to determine who receives your superannuation after you die. For some funds, such as industry super funds, the trustee is a big corporate entity, and for others like self-managed funds, the trustee is closer to home.

The range of eligible people to receive a superannuation death benefit is limited by legislation and the trust deed. The legislation limits beneficiaries to a dependant of the member, or the member's legal personal representative (the executor or administrator of your estate). A dependant includes:

- your spouse,

- any of your children, or

- any person that you have an interdependent relationship with.

A binding death benefit nomination can be used to tell your trustee where you want your superannuation paid after you die. This at least gives you a level of certainty that the trustee will pay your superannuation to the person you want it to go to. But remember that a binding death benefit nomination usually expires after three years, so you have to make sure that you keep it up to date!

If there is no binding death benefit nomination, the trustee may use its discretion to determine who will be the beneficiary of the superannuation death benefit. The trustee must determine all your current and ex-spouses, all your children, and anyone else you may be leaving behind who is dependent on you. The trustee will then look at the circumstances of each person, and the merits of paying all the benefit to one or another, or splitting the benefit between several potential beneficiaries.

If you have children who have started working, but don't have a spouse or children of their own, they cannot nominate their siblings or you as their parent. This would be an invalid nomination, and the trustee of the super fund could not follow it. This is crucial, since the death benefit on super is usually the biggest asset for young people. There are ways to get around this, so don't let them just put their heads in the sand!

It is also important to remember that there are often tax consequences on the distribution of superannuation. Only your spouse, and children under the age of 18 years old are usually exempt from tax on superannuation. So if you make a binding nomination with your superannuation trustee to pay your superannuation to your adult children, be aware that they will be taxed. Often the tax paid will be uneven because they are in difference tax brackets.

It may be best for you to make a binding nomination with your superannuation trustee to pay your superannuation death benefit to your legal personal representative, who is the executor or administrator of your estate. That way the superannuation is paid into your estate, and goes in accordance with your wishes under your Will. This can give you more control, and the estate will pay any tax on the superannuation. However, your superannuation then becomes part of your estate and is subject to family provision claims like any other asset

19.2 Who can I leave super to?

The superannuation legislation only allows you to leave your superannuation to a dependant, or your legal personal representative (your executor in your Will, so that you can disperse your superannuation under your Will). A dependant is your spouse, a child (of any age), or any other person in an interdependent relationship with you.

A spouse is someone with whom you live as husband or wife, whether you're married or not, and whether you're same-sex or not.

A child includes a step-child, an adopted child and an ex-nuptial child. It does not include a grandchild unless the grandchild has been adopted by you, even if the grandchild is being brought up by you as your own child.

So, you can see that these options are not suitable for everyone. A young person without a spouse or children may want to leave your superannuation to their parents. To do this, they must nominate their 'legal personal representative' to be their beneficiary on their nomination form. That way the superannuation will be paid into their estate, and then in their Will they would leave their superannuation to their parents.

If you are part of a blended family, you may want your superannuation to be left only to your own children, and not to your step-children. You would need to nominate your legal personal representative to be your beneficiary, so that the superannuation will be paid into your estate. Then in your Will you would leave your superannuation to your children. This could open another can of worms, though, if your Wills was disputed.

There are many other examples. So the advice is: you need to get individual advice about your superannuation and your estate.

19.3 Blended families - a case study

Mark and Jenny are married. Both of them had previous marriages, and Mark has two children from his previous marriage, Cara and Chris, who are now both adults. Jenny has a son, Lachlan, who is 12 years old and lives with her and Mark. They have no children together.

After his first divorce, Mark has very few assets. He was able to retain his superannuation with AustralianSuper, an industry super fund. He and Jenny have bought a house together, jointly owned, and mortgaged up to 70% of its value.

Mark has $600,000 in his superannuation fund, and has life and total permanent disability insurance cover for a further $750,000. He would like to divide his superannuation benefit between Jenny 60%, Cara 20% and Chris 20%. Remember, superannuation is not an estate asset that can be dealt with under a

Will, unless Mark makes a binding nomination that all his death benefit goes to his estate.

Without a binding nomination to AustralianSuper, the trustee of the super fund is likely to determine to leave the majority of the superannuation (if not all) to Jenny and Lachlan (as a financial dependent and step-child). If Mark wants to ensure Cara and Chris get some of the benefit, he will need to make a binding death benefit nomination. It is important to find out from AustralianSuper whether the binding nomination can be non-lapsing, or whether it lapses every 3 years and Mark needs to remember to redo it. There is a risk that the binding nomination would lapse if Mark forgets to redo the nomination, and his own children could miss out.

Of Jenny, Cara and Chris, only Jenny would be within the definition of a death benefit dependent for tax purposes. Cara and Chris would need to pay part of the benefit that they receive as tax, at the income tax rate that they otherwise earn. They may not each receive an equal amount after tax.

If Jenny died before Mark, Mark would like to have Lachlan receive part of the superannuation. But if Jenny was dead, then Lachlan would no longer be a 'child' of Mark (as he was only a step-child under the definition whilst his mother was alive). However, if Lachlan is still a minor and still living with Mark, then Lachlan would likely fall within the definition of a financial dependent instead, so Mark could nominate Lachlan in that situation.

Mark has given Jenny a power of attorney if he loses capacity. If he loses capacity, he could be entitled to the insurance cover associated with his benefit, under his total and permanent disability cover. Jenny, as his attorney, could withdraw from his fund on his behalf prior to his death. This would render the binding nomination either useless (depending on how much was withdrawn), or would significantly deplete the amount of money that his children would inherit. This would either be a risk that Mark would have to take, or he could prepare a Will with a specific gift clause that tracks any superannuation and ensures it is equalised between his children.

Chapter Twenty

Self-Managed Superannuation Fund ("SMSF"): Death and Incapacity

If you have a SMSF it is crucial that you think about who the executor is under your Will, and who you appoint under an enduring power of attorney, because they will exercise control over your super and retirement funds by controlling the trustee of your SMSF.

There were some important points and myths to be aware of:

What happens to my SMSF if I die?

- If there are two members of your self-managed super fund (ie. husband and wife), generally you will have a binding nomination to leave your super to your spouse. Therefore, your spouse would receive your part of the super fund, and the super fund would become a single-member super fund. There may be some compliance changes that need to be met for this to occur.

- If you are a member of a fund in which you do not leave your share to the surviving members, then your legal personal representative (executor under your Will or your administrator) usually steps into your shoes as trustee and receives your death benefit from the super fund to pay in accordance with your instructions.

- If you are in a single-member super fund, then your legal personal representative will become the trustee and will wind up the fund. This fund cannot be restricted - it must be wound up as soon as practicable.

Does the legal personal representative have to be appointed?

No, your legal personal representative is not compelled to act as the trustee. They could appoint someone else as a replacement director of a corporate trustee, for example. Or they could appoint an APRA approved Regulated Superannuation Entity to be the trustee.

What is the timeframe for payment of the death benefit from my SMSF?

This should happen as soon as practicable. But there is no strict time frame. The self-managed super fund will cease and therefore should be wound up within 6 months, unless an APRA approved Regulated Superannuation Entity is appointed.

What happens to my SMSF if I lose capacity?

If you lose capacity, hopefully you have executed an enduring power of attorney and appointed someone. 'Legal personal representative' is defined broadly for the purposes of SMSFs and includes people appointed under a power of attorney. So your attorney will step into your shoes as trustee and member (the fund will not fail).

If you haven't appointed someone under an enduring power of attorney, your family may have to seek an order from VCAT to appoint an Administrator. Although the legislation for SMSFs does not include Administrators as legal personal representatives, the Australia Tax Office has issued an Interpretative Decision in 2010 that in their view a legal personal representative also includes a VCAT appointed Administrator.

Where are the governing rules of your SMSF found?

There are detailed rules in legislation governing superannuation. However do you know where the specific rules for your self-managed super fund are found? In your trust deed.

Trust deeds are *not* a standard document. Although some deeds might be very similar, there are many versions of superannuation trust deeds out there. Therefore, your trust deed is unique to your self-managed super fund, and most of the rules for how it operates are found there.

Who can be a trustee of your self-managed superannuation fund?

Members must be the trustee of their self-managed super fund (up to 4), but a corporate trustee could be appointed. There must be at least two individual trustees unless there's a corporate trustee, so if there's only one member of the fund then another person needs to also be the trustee. A common scenario would be that a couple has a self-managed super fund, and one of the couple dies. The survivor is the only member of the fund left, but they cannot be the sole trustee. Another trustee needs to be appointed, even though they won't be a member of the fund!

A sole purpose corporate trustee is preferable for a number of reasons, including consistency, ease of administration changes, protection from creditors, and less opportunities for mistakes.

Who can be a shareholder of your self-managed superannuation fund corporate trustee?

Usually, the members have to be directors of the corporate trustee. However, there's absolutely no rule as to whom must own the shares in the company in order for the relevant fund to comply with the legislation requirements to be a self-managed super fund.

What does this mean to you? If you're concerned about the control of the super fund if you lose capacity or die, then you can have other strategic shareholders who have the power to appoint a director, so you can ensure who controls your super and therefore where it goes.

Chapter Twenty-One

Will Disputes

I've had a few more people than usual who have asked how to cut one of their children out of their Will. My answer is: not with absolute certainty.

In Australia, you have testamentary freedom, which is the freedom to make whatever Will you want. However, each State and Territory then puts some limitations on that freedom by giving certain people the ability to dispute a Will if they prove there was a moral obligation to them, and that they are in need of the inheritance. In July 2015, the laws in Victoria changed to narrow the range of people who can make a claim, but your children will still be in the category of those who can claim.

So regardless of how much you don't like one of your children, or how badly your relationship has broken down, or how long it has been since you've seen one of your children, you still have an obligation to provide for them, particularly if they need it.

Then I'm often asked: what is the minimum I can give them to prevent them from claiming under the Will? My answer is: there is no minimum. You cannot give someone a small amount of cash on condition that they don't claim against the Will. This works in some States in the USA, which is why people have heard of it, from watching TV. But that's not the law in Australia. If you leave a legacy to a child, and they don't think it's enough, they can claim against your Will.

So what solutions do I suggest?

The first is to cut them out, and give reasons in your Will. This won't necessarily prevent a claim, but it shows that you have thought about it and done it deliberately, for what you believe are good reasons. To back this up, I then suggest leaving detailed notes for your executor.

If a claim is made against your Will, the reason why so many are successful, is that the will-maker cannot defend their decision. They cannot give their evidence, so it ends up being the child's evidence against the executors (and the executor often doesn't have details). So, to help your executor win against a Will claim, you need to leave as much evidence behind that your executor can use. Write as much information down as you can, and let your executor use it in Court if they have to, otherwise it can remain confidential if no claim is made.

The other solution I suggest is that you can give as much away whilst you're alive as possible. If you don't own it when you die, then it doesn't form part of your estate. In Victoria, there are no claw back provisions, like there are in New South Wales. So, you're safe to get rid of your assets. You can do this by creating joint accounts with the children you want to inherit from you, or by transferring real estate into joint names. There are stamp duty consequences of doing this, but to spend some money upfront to protect the inheritance for the children you want it to go to is often worth it. A family trust could also be used.

Who can claim?

The legislation in Victoria in relation to family provision claims changed in 2015. The new changes have significantly restricted the people who can make a claim against your Will. This has been done by introducing a list of eligible people who can make a claim. The list includes:

- spouse

- children
- the spouse of your dead child, and
- a member of your household.

Spouse

Whether married or de facto, if you have a current spouse at the time of your death and you exclude them from your Will (or haven't updated it to include them) then they have a claim against your Will.

An ex-spouse can also make a claim against your Will, if a property settlement hasn't been finalised under the Family Law Act.

Children

If you exclude your children from your Will, they could also make a claim. Children who are under 18, disabled, or full-time students and under 25 have a fairly good chance of making a claim. Adult children who can stand on their own two feet financially have less of a chance, since the Court is coming down on such claims.

People who were treated as your children, and who believed they were your child for part of their lives, can also make a claim. This would encompass the category of a grandchild being raised as the grandparents' own child.

Step-children can also make a claim. Unfortunately, there is no definition as to what a step-child is. Does it only include a child who is raised in a blended family? Or does it also include adult children of a late second marriage? Does the deceased have to have married the new spouse, or can step-children include those of a de facto spouse? We can only wait to see how the Courts interpret the new legislation on this point. No doubt, each case will be dealt on its own merits.

Spouse of your dead child

If a child of yours died within 12 months of your death, then their spouse could make a claim against your Will.

Member of your household

A member of your household, whether they are a family member or not, could make a claim against your Will. They have to prove that they have been financially dependent on you.

Another similar category is someone who has a registered caring relationship with you. This is more than just a Centrelink carer - this relationship needs to be registered with Births Deaths and Marriages.

Chapter Twenty-Two

Estoppel

Part IV of the *Administration and Probate Act* is the primary means to bring a claim against a Will in Victoria - that is, a family provision claim, or testator's family maintenance claim, which was discussed in the previous chapter. Such a claim is that a family member who the deceased person had an obligation to provide for has not been given an adequate amount in the Will.

Another way of making a claim against a Will is a claim of estoppel. The doctrine of estoppel applies when a person expects to receive a gift in the Will, because of representations and promises that the deceased person has made to them. Because of those promises, the person went out of their way to rely on the promise, otherwise to their detriment. Then they don't get what they were promised despite having acted that way they did - the law won't let them miss out.

Make sure you don't make promises, even flippant ones, that you will 'leave everything' to someone, or they could rely on it!

In farming families, this is a perfect example. One child stays on the farm and earns less than market value in wages, on the promise that they will get the farm when the parents die. Instead, the parents leave the farm equally to their children, and the child who had stayed on the farm is disadvantaged because they relied on the promise.

To get an estoppel claim raised, there has to be reliance on the promise, and a detriment due to that reliance. The reliance also cannot have been unreasonable in the circumstances.

These cases are rare, but it will be interesting to see if they increase, given the changes to the laws in Victoria which now limit the categories of people who can make a family provision claim. Those excluded from the categories for a family provision claim may still make an estoppel claim.

Chapter Twenty-Three

Administration of an estate

22.1 What is probate?

I'm quite often asked: what is probate? A lot of people think that it is a tax, and that it's an amount that is paid depending on how big the estate is. Wrong.

In most States in Australia, the fee for probate is not related to the size of the estate at all. In Victoria, it is a flat fee to the Supreme Court - just a filing fee - and far cheaper than many other court applications that you could make.

Probate is just a legal document issued by the Supreme Court, confirming the validity of the Will, and giving the executor the legal right to deal with assets in the estate, particularly real estate.

A grant of probate is a grant of representation in a deceased estate when there is a Will. Letters of administration are the equivalent grant of representation in a deceased estate when someone dies intestate (without a valid Will).

To apply for probate, the executor(s) need to submit an application to the Supreme Court in the form of an Originating Motion, to commence proceedings. All the proceedings are usually dealt with without anyone having to appear, so it is all just paperwork.

The executor's evidence with their application is in the form of an affidavit. In the affidavit they need to establish that the person has died (usually by attaching the death certificate), they need to prove that the Will is valid, and they need to submit an inventory of the assets and liabilities of the estate.

Putting this application together can take a few weeks after the death certificate arrives, and in Victoria death certificates are taking 6-8 weeks to issue. So beneficiaries of an estate should expect that it will take about 3-4 months after the death before an application is made for probate.

Then, after probate, in most States, because Wills can be contested within 6 months of probate being granted, estates usually aren't distributed for another

6 months. So, generally an estate is finalised within 10 months at the earliest, but some estates can take years to administer.

22.2 Acting as executor

If you're serving as the executor of someone's estate, it may not be enough to read the provisions of the Will and follow what it says. Not only are there subtle terms of construction and jargon in Wills, but there may also have been external events that significantly affect how you distribute property under the Will.

Did the Will-maker separate or get divorced?

In Victoria, if someone gets divorced after making a Will, any gifts the Will makes to the former spouse, or any roles they are appointed for, are automatically revoked. The rest of the Will is still valid. For example, if the will you're working with leaves gifts to the deceased person's ex-spouse, you should proceed as if the former spouse had not survived the Will-maker. The property left to the ex-spouse will go to the alternative beneficiary named in the Will.

However, if the death occurred after the couple had separated but not yet divorced, this will not have any effect on the Will. Even though it's probable that the deceased person didn't want their property to go to their ex-spouse, the gift will still stand.

Have beneficiaries died before the Will-maker?

If the Will leaves property to someone who died before the Will-maker did (or within 30 days), you must figure out who inherits the property. Sometimes the Will tells you; in other cases, you must look to legislation.

If the Will names alternatives for the beneficiaries, it's clear what happens to the property if the first choice recipient doesn't meet the survivorship requirement: the alternative gets it.

If the Will does not name an alternative beneficiary, or the alternative beneficiary has also died, you have a lapsed or failed gift. Depending on the nature of the gift, the property will either form part of the residuary estate, or it might pass to the primary beneficiary's decedents under intestacy.

What if the lawyer who drafted the Will gets property under the Will?

Over the years, solicitors have been doing the wrong thing by giving themselves gifts from elderly and infirm clients in an embarrassingly large number. These gifts are often void. Even the appointment of a lawyer as the executor can be void, if they didn't meet their legal professional responsibilities of making proper disclosures to the Will-maker at the time of writing the Will. If you are a co-executor with a solicitor, make sure they met their legal professional obligations at the time the Will was drafted, or you could dispute their appointment to avoid their costs.

Property has been given away or sold

A long time may pass between the time a Will is signed and the death of the Will-maker. By the time the Will-maker dies, their assets might be very different from when they made the Will. For example, the Will-maker may have sold a house and moved into an apartment or nursing home, given away jewellery and cash, and sold the car.

Where specifically gifted property has been sold prior to the Will-maker's death then those gifts are usually "adeemed", meaning that the asset is gone so theft cannot be given. Where the Will-maker gives their own property away whilst they are alive, you cannot recover those gifts in Victoria. There are potentially some exemptions to ademption, but these would need to be closely investigated.

Beneficiaries have already received their inheritance

Beneficiaries aren't supposed to get a double share. If the Will-maker gives the beneficiary their inheritance whilst they are still alive, there are provisions in legislation to make sure they don't double dip under the Will as well. But the difficulty is to know whether the Will-maker meant the gift during their lifetime was supposed to be inheritance or not - usually there is nothing written, and the memories of family members will differ. It's not something that you would want to fight about in court, so if it can be worked out amongst the family this is always the best solution.

The Will-maker gave you different instructions

As you go through the deceased's personal papers, you may find notes that seem to set out different intended beneficiaries. Or the deceased person may have given you oral instructions that supplement or even contradict the Will. These notes, lists and oral requests are probably not legally binding, but it's always possible with the consent of all the beneficiaries to change the Will after the Will-maker dies, to give effect to these wishes that are not properly recorded, if everyone agrees.

Chapter Twenty-Four

Death and taxes

What most people actually mean when they ask "does probate still exist?" is "what taxes apply"?

Well, there are no death duties or estate taxes in Australia!

The taxes that apply to an estate after someone dies are mainly income tax, stamp duty and capital gains tax.

Income tax

A final tax return will often need to be done for the deceased individual, up until the date they die. If the estate earns any income before it is distributed to beneficiaries (like interest or dividends) then the estate may also need to do a tax return to pay income tax.

Stamp duty

If real estate is gifted to someone under a Will, then there is no stamp duty payable on the transfer of that land in Victoria.

If someone buys the real estate from the estate (even if that person was partially a beneficiary) then there is stamp duty paid by the purchaser, just like if they were purchasing any other property.

Capital gains tax

Generally, if real estate (or another capital asset) is gifted to someone under a Will, then there is also no capital gains tax payable, because the transfer doesn't amount to a disposal of an asset for CGT purposes.

However, what does change is the asset's cost base in the hands of the beneficiary when they come to sell the property. This is probably a good thing, because they don't inherit a low cost base if the deceased had owned the property for a while. The cost base is reset to the market value as at the date of death.

The main residence exemption on capital gains tax applies for two years after the date of death, so the estate can sell the property within that time and not incur capital gains tax.

Dealing with the capital gains tax for joint tenancies or life estates is too complex for this book, but is certainly something that professionals should help you with, if you are an executor of a Will.

Chapter Twenty-Five

Digital Assets, Facebook, Google and iTunes

It is important, particularly the younger generations, for will-makers to consider their digital assets. Most people have a Facebook account now, and other accounts where they upload videos or other files online or into 'the cloud'. If you want specific things to occur to your online accounts, you need to leave instructions and the necessary powers for this to happen. At the very least, people with online accounts should give their executors and attorneys the power to use, access and delete their online accounts, and to recover passwords if they need to do these things.

25.1 Facebook

When you die, Facebook used to give your family two options - either permanently delete the site, or make the site a memorial site. There were lots of issue involved with who had the authority to make that decision, and who would Facebook listen to?

The difficulty for solicitors acting for the estate of a deceased person is that they cannot activate the contact with Facebook themselves. Only a Facebook friend of the deceased is able to lodge the initial notification with Facebook.

According to Facebook's rules, you cannot leave your username and password for someone else to take over and control your page that way. No one else is allowed to log in as you.

You can appoint the person, directly with Facebook, that you want to control you Facebook page if you die. You can also choose to have your Facebook page permanently deleted upon Facebook being notified of your death.

Your legacy contact, once they have notified Facebook of your death, will then be given permission under this new feature to control your memorial page, and to download photos and posts from your archive.

Your legacy contact will be able to post a display at the top of the timeline on your memorial page - something to announce your memorial. They will be able to respond to new friend requests and update your profile picture and cover photo.

They will not be able to:

- review any private messages sent to you or your page (so these will effectively go unseen and unanswered;

- delete a picture or post that someone has put into your timeline, even if it is offensive; or

- remove any friends.

Arguably, these are some important features that you would want a legacy contact to have, so if your legacy contact cannot control access private messages, or remove distressing comments from your page (perhaps a troll is taunting your family after you die), then you might ask what is the point?

It may be preferable to have Facebook allow someone access to download all your photos and a memory of your timeline, and then delete the page. You have to wonder who consulted with Facebook in the introduction of this feature.

25.2 Google, iTunes, Amazon and others

Google has a similar process, where you can appoint a Google Inactive Account Manager who would have limited access to your account to wind it down, if your account has been inactive for a certain period, and you are presumed to have deceased.

Accounts like iTunes and other services where you can buy music, movies, ebooks and TV shows are usually licensed services. These are *not* like an online service where you save you own material, like Dropbox or Instagram. Instead, when you use a service like iTunes you enter a service agreement with them to purchase or rent a license for the digital content.

Your account is not transferrable, and cannot be assigned to someone else. It should be automatically shut down as soon as the service is notified that you die. Also, almost all services requiring a password have a condition in their agreement that you must not share your password with anyone else.

Apple uses its Digital Rights Management system to monitor how many times you share the music or other products you are licensed to use. You can share with up to 5 other computers. You are also allowed to copy the music or other digital content onto external drives, burn them onto CDs or DVDs, or convert the format. This is probably the way to save the content of your iTunes account, instead of it all disappearing when you die.

You won't want to upload too much money or gift cards into your iTunes account, either. Unused funds in your iTunes account are not redeemable for cash, and not transferable to another account.

Services like Amazon or Microsoft are more strict with their online licensed products. For example, if you have a Kindle device and you're collecting lots of ebooks, you can't transfer them or pass them onto someone else.

So what can you do? Well, there aren't any complete solutions:

1. you can leave your physical devices to someone. But, as you know, access to your account is needed to keep up with updates. If updates aren't done regularly, then the device becomes vulnerable and the new owner could lose everything. Within a couple of years the device could be obsolete, and there's no way of transferring the content;

2. you could hand over your passwords to your accounts to your next of kin. This sounds simple, and probably what most people do. But it's actually a breach of the terms and conditions of your account. So if someone logs in and pretends to be you, they are committing a security breach - Apple or the service provider could terminate the account completely and ban your next of kin;

3. with Apple content, you can at least share it with other users and burn it onto other devices or formats, so long as it's only ever for personal use. This option is not available for all license service providers;

4. your next of kin could plead with the service provider after you've passed away, for them to give them temporary access to your account. This will work to enable them to burn content, so that they can save it. But accounts cannot be transferred, so it would only be a temporary measure; or

5. it's a relatively new field, and not many solicitors are doing it, but you could have specific bequests in your Will about your online accounts. This is a developing area of law that still has to be properly tested over many of the service providers. But many of the service providers will recognise a gift or bequest of some forms of ownership. iTunes, Amazon and other license services remains an uncertainty due to the limitations on transferring accounts and non-ownership of the content. Stay tuned!

6. the next phase of online services seems to be iTunes radio, Pandora and other temporary services where you don't buy a license to a specific content, but have a recurring account payment just to access a huge amount of material. There's no confusion about owning anything here - you are hiring access. All your family needs to do is cancel the recurring payment if you die.

Chapter Twenty-Six

More Case Studies

26.1 Single parents

Sara, a single mother working part-time, with her pre-school children both in day care, had a car accident on the way to pick her kids up. She was trapped in the vehicle, with crush wounds to her legs, and a concussion. Emergency crews took hours to get her out of the vehicle and get her to hospital. Her phone was broken in the accident, and she didn't have anything in her purse to indicate who her next of kin were or where her children were.

When she was late to collect her children from day care, the centre called her mother who was listed as the contact in case of emergency. Sara's parents lived 3 hours away, but her mother didn't answer the phone because they were away on a holiday. The father of Sara's children wasn't suitable, so Sara hadn't listed him as a contact. The last resort for the day care centre was to call the police. The police took the children, and were able to determine that Sara was in hospital. They couldn't find any other carers for the children, so they went into emergency foster care.

Is this what you would want for your children? If you haven't planned for this circumstance, then who's to say that the police and child protection services won't get involved?

Sara's accident could have been worse. If she had died in the accident, she didn't have a Will, so she hadn't appointed guardians for her children. The father of her children would have automatically become the sole guardian of her children, and he would have cut her family out of their lives, causing an ongoing court battle for Sara's parents to see the children.

Without a Will, Sara's children would inherit her estate once they turned 18 years of age. In the meantime, it is likely that the father of her children would have had control of the estate as their guardian. This is not what Sara would have wanted. She would have wanted her parents to be in control of her estate, and for her sister to have been the guardian of her children. She would have wanted her children to inherit the estate at 25 years of age, or older.

The plans and preparations made today could impact generations to come, and it is quick and easy to do the right thing for the people you love most. Best to take action while you can, and not have to us the plan, rather than leave it up to chance.

26.2 Blended family

Jay needs to do his Will and estate plan. He and Gloria are married, but Jay has two adult children from his first marriage, Claire and Mitchell. Gloria has one child from a previous relationship, Manny aged 10, who lives with her and Jay. Jay and Gloria have just had a baby together, Joe.

Most of the assets of the couple are held in Jay's name, and include a business, a house, bank accounts and motor vehicles to the value of $10,000,000. Jay also has a self-managed superannuation fund valued at $1,000,000. He has no life insurance, but has no debt.

These are the factors he needs to consider:

Executors

Jay needs to think about who would be best as executors. Gloria alone could be the executor, if she survives Jay, but it depends on how the estate is structured. It may be more beneficial to have more than one executor, because there are minor children to consider, being both Manny and Joe.

Guardians for children

If Gloria and Jay die together, consideration needs to be given to a guardian for Joe and Manny. Gloria wants to make sure that Manny stays in the country and doesn't return to South America, and she wants to make sure that Manny and Joe are together. So the best options for guardians are Jay's adult children. Neither of them really mind if it is Claire and her husband, or Mitchell and his husband, that care for the children. But their primary concern is that their children are in a stable home with other children and that their guardians won't go through a divorce.

Beneficiaries

Jay has many people who he has an obligation to provide for. He needs to take into account family provision legislation that allows a family member to make a claim against his Will if they are not sufficiently provided for. Gloria, his wife, would have the best claim if she was not adequately provided for. But Jay also has to manage the interests of his adult children from his first marriage. He also needs to ensure that his baby is provided for, and he needs to consider to what extent he provides for Manny, his step-son. Should Manny be treated equally to his own natural children?

Superannuation

Superannuation is not an estate asset, so needs to be dealt with separately. There are three primary categories of people that superannuation can be given to: spouse, children, or legal personal representative (filtered through the Will via the executor). Jay needs to consider whether he leaves a reversionary beneficiary to the pension in his superannuation fund, or whether he should leave a direction for the payment of a lump sum from his superannuation fund. He also needs to think about the tax treatment on the super fund, as Gloria and Joe won't be taxed, but his adult children would be.

Business succession

Jay also needs to consider what will happen with his business on his death. Has a strategy to make sure the business continues if he dies been put in place? Does he have key-person insurance in his business for himself? Is there a business partner and should they enter into a buy-sell agreement?

What Jay decides to do:

He appoints Gloria and Mitchell as his executors, with Claire as the back-up in case either Gloria or Mitchell predecease Jay.

Then Jay gives a $250,000 legacy to Mitchell and Claire, and leaves the balance of the estate on a life interest for Gloria to use. She has the house to live in, and she has the interest income from the investments to live off. Jay also puts Gloria down as his binding nomination on his superannuation fund, so she will also get the $1,000,000 in super assets. On the death of Gloria, the estate gets split 4 ways, to go equally to Mitchell, Claire, Manny and Joe.

If either Mitchell or Claire (or Manny or Joe) predecease, leaving children (Jay's grandchildren), then those children would get the share their parent would have got, once they reach twenty-five years.

In the event that Gloria predeceases Jay, Claire and Phil will be guardians for Manny and Joe. Mitchell and Cam would become guardians if either Claire or Phil predeceased, or if they separated.

If Gloria has predeceased, then the whole estate gets split into four equal parts and goes to Mitchell, Claire, Manny and Joe.

Manny and Joe have to be twenty-five before they can inherit anything in either scenario, so funds will be held on trust by the executors until they reach that age.

26.3 Same sex couple

Mitchell and his partner, Cameron, live together with their young adopted daughter, Lily. They are modestly wealthy, their home being worth $800,000 with a $250,000 mortgage remaining. They each have superannuation of approximately $200,000 and life insurance each of $500,000.

In Australia, Mitchell and Cameron would be recognised as spouses, in case they didn't have a Will. Also, their adopted daughter is considered a natural child of theirs under the laws dealing with estates. If Mitchell or Cameron died intestate, then the laws of intestacy would apply, such that the surviving spouse would get the first $100,000, and then the remaining estate would be divided 1/3 to the spouse and 2/3 to Lily. Lily would inherit at eighteen years old.

However, Mitchell and Cameron do want to ensure their estate planning is done. They need to consider who would be the executors of the estate in the case that both of them have passed away, given that the funds would be held in trust for Lily. They also need to think about who would be suitable to be Lily's guardian. They need to consider who will benefit if they all pass away together in an accident, and they also need to consider that if one of them should die, the other may re-partner.

Mitchell and Cameron decide to appoint Mitchell's sister Claire and her husband, Phil, as guardians for Lily. However, their decision for executor is more difficult. In the instance that one of them dies, they appoint each other. But in the event that they've both passed away, they are conscious that Claire and Phil shouldn't also be the executors, to safeguard Lily's inheritance. They really want Mitchell's father Jay as one of the executors, but he is obviously a generation older and should pass before them in the natural order of things. Despite this concern, they end up appointing Jay and Claire as the alternative executors, because Jay is relatively healthy and should reach an age for Lily to be old enough to inherit.

After their house, which is jointly owned so will automatically transfer to the survivor of them, their biggest asset is their respective superannuation accounts. Because they want to control where their superannuation is paid, they decide to nominate that the superannuation should be paid into their estate, to their legal personal representative, and then they can deal with their superannuation in their Will.

Mitchell and Cameron decide that their superannuation should be used to pay out the mortgage, and then $200,000 should go into trust for Lily until she reaches twenty-five years old. The balance can be paid to the surviving spouse. This ensures that Lily will get something, if either of them re-partner and end up leaving the balance of their estate to their new partner.

In the event that both of them pass away, Mitchell and Cameron confirm that the entire estate should form a testamentary trust for Lily, which she will control once she reaches the age of twenty-five years. Until then, Claire and Jay will be trustees of that trust. Such a trust will protect Lily's inheritance from any future financial problems that she may suffer from, and also protect it from any future spouse of hers as well.

Finally, if Mitchell, Cameron and Lily all die together, they decide that they should split their combined estate in half. Half would be paid equally to Cameron's siblings, and half would be paid to Mitchell's siblings, being Claire and his new baby brother Joe once he reaches the age of twenty-five years.

26.4 Well-off nuclear family

Phil and Claire are married. They have three children, two to whom are still minors; Hayley, Alexis and Lucas. Most of their assets are jointly held: their house and bank accounts. Phil has a thriving real estate business in his own name. The total value of their assets are $5,000,000 including superannuation. Phil also has a $500,000 life insurance the total and permanent disability insurance cover.

If either Phil or Claire were to die, their joint assets would automatically transfer to the survivor. They do binding death benefit nominations with their superannuation funds for the funds to be paid into their estate, and then they leave everything to each other via a testamentary trust (instead of outright, to obtain the tax benefits and asset protection).

If both Phil and Claire die, they decide to appoint Jay and Mitchell as their executors. They nominate Jay and Gloria to be the guardians of their minor children. Jay has a very good business brain, but because there are minor children there should be more than one executor. Mitchell is preferable as the other executor instead of Gloria, because Mitchell will add a control and balance to Jay. If Jay and Gloria were both executors and guardians, there is room for foul play.

Phil and Claire decide to put $500,000 aside into an education trust for their children. The vesting date for the trust is after Luke attains the age of 25 years. After vesting, the balance remaining gets divided equally amongst the children (into their trusts). But this ensures that money is set aside to be used for education.

The balance of their joint estate would be left equally to their children in individual testamentary trusts that they would be able to control from the age of 25 years. Until that time, Jay and Mitchell will control their trusts.

Usual provisions are included in their Wills that if any of their children predecease them, leaving children, then their children (Phil and Claire's grandchildren) would take the share that their parent would have otherwise taken. If a child of theirs dies without have had children, then the estate just gets divided between the surviving children.

They also make provision for an accident in which all of them should die, as they do regularly travel together. Phil and Claire would want half of their estate to go to Mitchell and Joe (Clair's minor half-sibling), and the other half to Phil's siblings equally.

Going through this process with Phil and Claire has also raised issues as to what would happen with Phil's business if he were to die. Is Claire capable of running the business until she can sell it, or are there employees who can run the business whilst Claire maintains ownership? Phil may need to consider key-person insurance for the business, so that Claire could hire someone to take his place until she can come up with a solution.

Chapter Twenty-Seven

How Do I Talk to My Parents?

I am often asked "How can I talk to my parents about their estate plan ... without seeming like a gold-digger/control freak/I'm eager for them to be gone?"

Well, the short answer is: it's difficult. It's a very private and touchy subject in some families, where as other families are very open about these things. Some families don't like to disclose financial information, or what assets are owned, or how much debt there is. There's also another aspect to your parents' willingness to discuss things with you, and that is them not wanting to play favourites. They may not want to single out one of their children as the most responsible, or least trustworthy, or anything else. They want to keep their opinions of each of their children private.

Many people feel their estate plans are very personal and they don't want to talk about it. And that's ok. They are not obligated to tell you anything about their planning at all.

However, there are aspects of our parents' planning that are important to enquire about as they do affect you and your family directly. You can ask your parents some questions, without them revealing more than they are comfortable with sharing:

Have they done their estate planning?

Even this question can be difficult to ask, because your parents may feel like you have an ulterior motive in asking this question. It might be easier to frame this question by asking "Have you prepared Powers of Attorney as well as Wills?". Or you could lead by example and bring it up because you have just completed your own estate planning!

It's important to make sure that they've done Wills as well as made plans for their ageing and eventual declining health - what happens if they become incapacitated? It's also important to ascertain that they haven't cheaped-out on their plan to the point that it won't work.

If it's been more than five years since they've last reviewed their estate pan with their lawyer, you should suggest that they make an appointment to review it with their solicitor - to make sure that it still works the way they want it too, and see if circumstances have changed. Laws also change regularly, and this year there are a couple of major chances in Victorian law. An estate plan is not a set-and-forget endeavour. It's something to review every five years or so, to make sure it still works.

Am I or one of my siblings serving as an attorney or executor in your plan?

Feelings can get hurt when one adult child is serving and others are left out, sometimes bringing to the surface long dormant rivalries. Be mature yourself, and remember if you haven't been appointed in a role that your parents probably had a difficult choice about who to use and who to exclude.

If there are serious rivalries that you are aware of, that your parents aren't aware of or that they minimise, you might want to suggest that it be taken out of everyone's hands and given to a professional to save arguments and litigation.

Make sure that your parents have told any other siblings that have been appointed in a role, and what their role is. Suggest to your parents that it would be helpful to you (if any role that you have), and your siblings, to meet with their solicitor to learn what their obligations are in each role.

If I am inheriting something, is it protected from my creditors?

If you are in business, it may be preferable for you not to receive your inheritance directly, but for it to be held in a trust for you. Equally, if you are worried about your relationship breaking down, or just don't want your spouse to have any access to your inheritance, you will want to receive your inheritance into a well set up trust.

Some parents will want to make sure their hard-earned savings and assets are maximised for you. Other parents might want their children to suffer the consequences of their actions, and don't mind if their inheritance is lost due to poor financial decisions. Whichever way your parents decide, it will be good for your to know.

Asking this question could also prompt your parents to say they don't know, which means they should go back and see their solicitor again. They may not have explored these options with their solicitor, or have known it was important to you.

Will my children inherit anything?

Your parents may want to leave a legacy to your children, or they may want to skip a generation.

Either way, it would be good to know, and to make sure that their plan doesn't undercut your authority with your children. Discuss with your parents what age your children should inherit, and who should be in charge of its control in the meantime.

What are your wishes and plans if you need long term care?

We are living longer and longer, and our bodies are often out-living our minds. Have your parents set aside enough resources to pay for their care? Remember, our parents may need every last dime they have to support their lives until their last breath. You should have the discussion with them and the family home may need to be sold to pay for this, and they shouldn't expect that the home will be kept in the family.

Their wishes as to how they should be cared for, and what treatment they want to receive in certain situations should be recorded. It is better to have a record of what they want, rather than wondering once it's too late. An Advanced Healthcare Directive or a similar document should be part of their estate plan, along with the appointment of a medical attorney.

Here's the best advice: Expect nothing and you won't be disappointed.

How Much Does It Cost?

A Will is like everything else – you get what you pay for.

Asking "how much does a Will cost?" is a lot like asking "how much does a house cost?". There is no simple answer. The cost of a Will is dependant on a number of factors.

When making a Will, you are dealing with your legacy, and often hundreds of thousands of dollars of assets. So your Will deserves the appropriate attention, and not just skimping to get something down on paper that will be completely unsatisfactory in the long run. A poorly done Will can be worse than no Will at all.

Will kits: up to $50 ea

Will kits are available for many newsagency's, and are often given away for free as a bonus with other purchases in the finance and insurance industries.

Will kits may be suitable in a limited number of situations, but if you have children, they are unlikely to meet your needs. Will kits don't fully explain everything that a person should know before making their Will. It won't explain the relationship between your Will and your superannuation, nor will it explain who could make a claim against your Will and how to protect against that.

Mistakes are often made in meaning, and also in signing it correctly. These mistakes can cost thousands or even tens of thousands of dollars if you die and the Will kit needs to be relied on.

So Will kits are rarely the preferred option. You should spend a bit more now to save thousands later.

Internet Wills: up to $150 ea

These are similar to Will kits, though they are produced by entering details online and then you get the resulting document produced. If no solicitor is overseeing the process and contacting you for specific instructions and to give you advice, then you just have a standardised kit which again cannot give you specific advice for your circumstances.

All the same problems can arise with these forms of standardised Wills as they can from Will kits.

Simple Wills: from $200 ea

Solicitors can do a simple Will for you from as little as $200. This may be reduced during special promotions, such as Law Week, or through the Salvation Army that have lawyers help with their Will Day.

A simple Will would involve appointing an executor, and usually leaving all the residue of your estate to your spouse or someone else, and then a gift over clause in case that person dies. There would be some basic trustee powers as well. But the simple Will would not include specific gifts, it probably won't deal specifically with your superannuation, it wouldn't allow you to deal with assets individually, and wouldn't include any other special rights or options for beneficiaries.

If your circumstances are very simple, then a solicitor prepared simple Will is your best option. However, you may think that your circumstances are simple until you get advice from a solicitor.

You should be prepared that a simple Will is not appropriate for you at all.

Blended Family Wills: from $300 ea

As soon as your family situation is not straight forward, your Will needs more attention than a simple will. A second marriage, children to more than one spouse, a de facto partner, or even if you have a family business that some of the children are involved in but not others – these are circumstances that need some special attention with a solicitor who has appropriate knowledge and experience.

A solicitor will have strategies, and tricks and tips, to achieve special bequests and arrangements in your Will to make sure that you leave the legacy that you want. You don't want your family to be fighting after you're gone, so spend the time and money to get it right.

Testamentary Trusts: from $550 ea

If you want to set up a complex trust in your Will for your children, to protect your assets and give your children the benefits of incoming splitting and tax effective planning, then be prepared to spend more.

I recommend that most parents have testamentary trusts for their children, as the cost of setting it up will be worth it in the long run. If both you and your spouse die, then a testamentary trust is often the best you can do for your kids, and whilst there are some ongoing costs in running the testamentary trust, the tax savings can make it worthwhile.

Other factors

The cost of a Will will also depend on how your solicitor charges. If they charge on an hourly rate, and you need a number of appointments to complete your Will, then you will pay more for it. If you see a solicitor that gives you a fixed fee, be prepared that the fee may change if your circumstances are more complex than originally thought.

Finally, you are often paying for the experience and qualifications of your solicitor, and also their brand. Firms in the CBD of a capital city will charge a premium just for their location and prestige. A solicitor who is a certified specialist will charge more, because you can expect that you would get more complex legal advice and complex drafting in the Will.

Conclusion

This book really doesn't need a conclusion, because if you have elderly parents and adult children, potentially with children of their own, then by now you would have seen the importance of every generation having their estate planning sorted out.

You are the sandwich generation. You are the generation stuck between the other two. You are the responsible one, looking after everyone else. You are torn between them. You have obligations to both of them, and you thought you'd have some freedom by now! Just when your children should be grown up and gone, your parents decline and you need to keep an eye on them.

Take control. Talk to your parents and your children about their planning. If needed, make the appointments for them and impart your new-found knowledge.

This book was designed so you could read the relevant chapters when you needed them, and return to others as the scenarios arise, or situations change. You are now armed with the knowledge you need to ensure that life (and death) progresses as smoothly as possible, and increasing the potential for wealth protection and security.

This book is your guide about everything you need to know, about estate planning for yourself, as well as what you need to make sure your parents and children consider. This book will give you a great starting point to be able to seek out the further advice and guidance to get your planning done properly - and to make sure life is easier for everyone.

If you want more specific advice, then you are welcome to contact me, Jacqui Brauman, via my law firm TBA Law.

About the Author

Jacqui Brauman is the principal solicitor of TBA Law. Accredited Specialist in Wills and Estates, Jacqui's career of over 10 years in the legal industry has taken her from Central Victoria to rural New South Wales, to Sydney, and back to the outskirts of Melbourne.

Public school educated, Jacqui has been able to obtain a Bachelor of Laws, Bachelor of Accounting, Advanced Diploma in Taxation Law, and a Masters in Applied Law (Wills and Estates).

Jacqui has written and published two other legal books; "In Case of Emergency", and "Death and Social Media". She has also written "The Cult of Dissatisfaction", focusing on empowering unhappy professional women to make a change.

Jacqui is a member of the Law Institute of Victoria, the Society of Trust and Estate Practitioners, Victorian Women Lawyers, Rotary, HerBusiness, Business in Heels, the UN Women National Committee of Australia, and Professional Speakers Australia.

Schedule 1 - Business Succession Planning Checklist

BUSINESS SUCCESSION PLANNING CHECKLIST

Done	Date	Task
		Potential Successors
		Business Partner / Shareholder
		Family Member
		Employee
		Competitor
		Outsider
		Family Priorities
		Harmony
		More time
		Create family legacy
		Other:
		Personal Priorities
		Comfortable retirement income
		Minimise taxes
		Maximise philanthropy and community involvement

BUSINESS SUCCESSION PLANNING CHECKLIST

Done	Date	Task
		Preserve wealth for children/grandchildren
		Spend everything
		Ensure business survival
		Never retire
		Always be needed
		Your health
		Other:
		Retirement
		When?
		Full or partial retirement?
		Need capital or income?
		Safe to leave capital in business?
		Insurance funding?
		Superannuation or pension plan?
		Death or Disability
		Who takes over?
		How does your business continue?

BUSINESS SUCCESSION PLANNING CHECKLIST

Done	Date	Task
		Tax liability
		Insurance funding
		Spouse/family free from dependence on business?
		Business Topics
		Sole trader
		Partnership
		Unit or family trust
		Company
		Small business capital gains tax exempt?
		Debt insured?
		Key person insurance?
		Shareholder agreement/Partnership agreement/Buy-Sell agreement in force?
		Shareholder Agreement/Buy-Sell agreement
		Signed?
		Valuation procedure
		Triggering events defined?
		Cross purchase or repurchase

BUSINESS SUCCESSION PLANNING CHECKLIST

Done	Date	Task
		Provision for disability?
		Exposure to creditors
		Correct parties included?
		Include all classes of shares
		Tax Issue
		Income tax
		Capital gains tax
		Stakeholders to Consult
		Employees
		Family members
		Suppliers
		Customers
		Lenders
		Advisors
		Shareholders